GLOUCESTER CITY LIBRARIES

TELEPHONE 20020

Hours of opening from 2 September, 1957
Monday to Friday, 9.30 a.m. to 8 p.m.
Saturday, 9.30 a.m. to 7 p.m.
Wednesday, 9.30 a.m. to 1 p.m.

No. 6765 8

Due for return on or before the last date marked below.

23 DEC	10 A	7 NOV	30 DEC
21 JAN	20 NOV	21 NOV	
8 FEB	20. DEC		19 MAR
25 FEB	27 JAN		15 JAN
20 MAR	2 JUL		
29 MAR	13 JUL 31 OCT		20 APR
	8 DEC		
13 MAY	27 JUL		

Renewals. Provided that it is not required by another borrower, any book may be renewed by telephone or post-card, or by returning the book to the library.

Fines. Unless previously renewed a fine will be charged on this book in accordance with the scale of charges exhibited in the Libraries.

Borrowers' Tickets. Readers must notify the staff in case of change of address, or loss of ticket.

Infectious disease. Books must not be taken into any house in which there is a case of infectious disease. Books which have been exposed to infection must not be returned to the library, but must be handed to the Public Health Department.

Reservations and Suggestions. Please consult the staff if you are unable to find the book which you require.

Loss or damage. A charge will be made for any book lost or damaged. Borrowers are requested to call attention to any fau...

J.36355

MASTERS OF BRITISH DRAMA

MASTERS OF
BRITISH DRAMA

by

JOHN ALLEN

LONDON : DENNIS DOBSON

© 1957 by John Allen

FIRST PUBLISHED IN GREAT BRITAIN IN 1957
BY DOBSON BOOKS LTD,
80 KENSINGTON CHURCH STREET, LONDON, W 8
ALL RIGHTS RESERVED
PRINTED BY BRISTOL TYPESETTING CO, STOKES CROFT, BRISTOL

Contents

Contents.

Illustrations

ILLUSTRATIONS—*continued*

The following plates are reproduced by courtesy of the Victoria and Albert Museum: III, V, VI, VII, VIII, X, XVI, XVII, XVIII, XIX, XX, XXII

A description of all the plates will be found on pages 179-186

CHAPTER ONE

Reading and Seeing Plays

THIS IS A book about plays and the men who have written them. I hope you enjoy the book. But I hope even more that it will lead you to read plays and to see them performed whenever you have the opportunity. If you are already in the habit of reading and seeing plays, then I hope it will serve to increase your interest in the theatre and your understanding of some of the people who work for it.

Roughly speaking one can do three things about a play : see it acted, which is right and proper—but you have to be lucky to have a theatre near you; read it—if you are willing to take the trouble to get a printed copy; or act it— which is admirable but requiring no end of energy. This book is devoted to the first two alternatives, not because I am lazy but because that happens to be my subject.

So the first thing to do is to get the theatre-going habit, to become an intelligent theatre-goer, not just someone with a couple of favourite stars and their photos on the wall above your bed; but a serious discriminating sup- porter of what is called 'the living theatre', choosing with care what plays you are to visit, watching them attentively, and criticizing them with an informed judgment.

The second thing is to get into the way of reading plays, which usually means going to a public library and finding

9

your way to the book you want, blowing the dust off it, and recognizing that moment of triumph when the precious book is safely between your hands.

In this chapter I'm going to say one or two things about the theatre in general and reading and seeing plays in particular. I can't tell you what constitutes a good play because I don't know; and nor does anybody else. Some enthusiasts have had a try at formulating rules but the only decent thing to do with a rule is to break it. In art anyway. And that's what the dramatists have done.

One thing I can say with certainty is that dramatists write plays to be performed. I do not know of a single dramatist who has been satisfied at the publication of his play if it had not already been, or was not about to be, performed. The reason is simply that if he had wanted to write a story he would have done so in the form of a story; for a play is a story that is *acted* which is quite a different thing from a story that is *told*. It is only necessary to read a few pages of a novel and then of a play to understand why the novel is far more suitable for reading than a play.

But for all that, plays are published and are often very readable. A dramatist like Bernard Shaw, for instance, who was extremely anxious that his plays should be read as well as seen, published them with full and carefully-written stage-directions. This was a very smart move on his part for copies of his plays have been sold in enormous numbers throughout the world. The plays of William Shakespeare, on the other hand, are difficult to read until one gets used to them because they have very few stage directions. Shakespeare himself, as a matter of fact, wrote almost none at all. He did not even divide his plays into acts and scenes. Most of that kind of donkey-work has been done by editors who have tried to make the plays clear to people reading them for the first time.

The upshot of this is that a would-be dramatist hasn't got to follow a lot of rules, beyond a few that are obvious and common-sensical; but he must be able to create living characters, or characters that can be brought to life by reasonably good actors, simply by means of what he puts into their mouths to say. Once he has acquired the details of technique that I would lump together as 'a sense of the theatre' everything else will follow without much more trouble.

It is this same sense of the theatre that has to be acquired by anyone who is going to enjoy reading plays. As one reads one must learn to hear the dialogue and see the characters vividly in the mind's eye. This, strangely, is an exceedingly rare faculty even among people who have worked in the theatre all their lives, and the reason is that however clearly one visualizes a play in performance, it is extremely difficult to know how the actors are going to interpret it. Actors are not Protean creatures, infinitely capable of changing their personalities, and producers who are excessively imperative in their demands some-times destroy their confidence. Acting is not an exact art and there is always a bit of a gamble in the production of a play.

This difficulty of envisaging what a play is going to be like in performance is often very unfortunate, for learned people especially are inclined to criticize plays, particularly those which for various reasons are not often performed, for being poor literature when in fact they are magnificent drama. I shall give a good many examples of this in the course of this book—as well as of plays that contain fine language but which are rotten drama.

The ideal way of judging the work of a dramatist is to go and see his plays on the stage whenever possible. Unfortunately the number of theatres in Great Britain is dwindling while the cost of theatre-going rises. To those people who are ready to complain about the cost of a seat in the theatre as compared with a seat in the cinema I would like to point out that you can still get a decent theatre seat for fifteen shillings. The same seat in the eighteen-sixties, nearly a hundred years ago, would have been ten shillings. Thus while the cost of a theatre seat has increased about fifty per cent, the cost of putting on plays has increased astronomically, and out of all proportion. This does not mean that fifteen shillings is not really a lot of money to pay for a decent seat in the theatre; but it does mean that the modern theatre has failed to adapt itself to the tastes of the millions who drowse into their television sets nightly and visit the cinema weekly. Obviously I can't go into this difficult question deeply in a book such as this; but I shall return to the subject in the last chapter when we have seen what exactly the British dramatists have offered us.

The problem of making a theatre pay its way has always been difficult and is now acute. This makes the theatre managers chary of taking risks. They dare not stage a play that may fail to draw large audiences even if they think it a good play. (Pessimism, for example, is always thought to be an extremely unpopular ingredient in a play; this would make *Timon of Athens* the most unpopular play ever written, but it would be disastrous if it were never produced.) Unhappily there are many fine plays in existence

which are rarely performed because they do not draw large
audiences. The reason for this is fairly simple. People's
tastes, thank goodness, vary. Millions of people read the
Daily Mirror every day and a couple of hundred thousand
read *The Times*. This does not mean that the *Mirror* is a
masterpiece of daily journalism and *The Times* is a
bit of a flop. It merely means that there are many more
Mirror-minded people than *Times*-minded people, just
as there are many more people ready to see Jane
Russell at the Gaumont Cinema than Paul Rogers at the
Old Vic.

But that is not the whole story. Many successful modern
novels sell twenty or thirty thousand copies soon after they
have been published and then, as like as not, are rarely
heard of again. They are a nine days wonder. But the great
classics of literature sell three or four hundred copies a year
for centuries perhaps. A publisher will be quite contented
with this slow and steady sale. But theatres are organized
differently. Everyone likely to be interested in a certain
play must be induced to see it within a very few weeks.
Each year a few hundred copies of the plays of Ben Jonson,
Congreve, and Sheridan are sold in cheap editions. But if a
manager presents a play by one of these dramatists, and in
doing so has laid out as much money as the publisher has
spent in printing several thousand copies of the play, he
must get his theatre-goers to come along without delay.
And if they only number several thousand, he must get
them to come within a few days. The risk is considerable.
So what happens? Some of the great masterpieces of
English literature, the plays of Ben Jonson, for example,
are very rarely revived : *Volpone,* written in 1605, has been
revived in London fifteen times; *The Silent Woman*

(1609) eleven, *The Alchemist* (1610) sixteen, and *Bartholomew Fair* (1614), seven. Of the plays of Dryden, *All for Love* has been revived once since 1790, *Marriage à la Mode,* a lovely play, four times since 1675, and the great comedy *Love for Love* by Congreve only fifteen times since its first performance in 1695.

When the British public gets around to building itself a National Theatre, an undertaking in which most decent citizens appear to be sublimely disinterested, one of its main tasks will be to keep the little-played masterpieces of dramatists like Marlowe, Chapman, Jonson, Dryden, and Congreve in front of the public. This can be done very simply by adopting the 'repertory' system, which pertains in most opera houses. A company has a repertory, at any one time, of about a dozen pieces, some popular, some much less so; the programme is arranged so that the popular ones are given perhaps five times a week, and the less popular at the remaining performances. In this way the company will cater for a wide range of tastes, and the popular performances will 'support', as we say, the less popular.

I now want to say a few words about performances in general. Most people are aware, I imagine, that to stage a play, even a simple one, is a considerable undertaking. From the moment when the playwright has finished polishing the last syllable of his manuscript to the desperately anxious moment when the curtain rises for the first time on the first performance, a great number of highly skilled people will have made their contribution : a manager (who provides the theatre), a producer (who directs the whole ensemble), a designer (both of scenery and costumes), a composer perhaps, a company of actors, and a grand array of carpenters, painters, electricians, sempstresses, dress-makers, and musicians. And any single one of these specialists can wreck the ensemble. The dramatist, seeing his play at its first performance, may glow with pride and fancy himself an even cleverer fellow than he had thought himself to be; or he may fail to recognize his play as the one he wrote and vow that manager, producer, and actors have formed a pact to destroy his masterpiece and he'll starve before he writes another play. History is full of examples of both reactions. Between typescript and performance a play can be made or marred. Poor plays are sometimes so finely staged that they appear to be far better than they are. Two of the greatest successes of Sir Henry Irving, *The Bells* and *The Lyons Mail,* are laughably stupid to read. Yet it is clear that Irving transformed them into unforgettable theatrical experiences. On the other hand plays can be so badly performed that their finest qualities are lost. Unfortunately this happens so often that it is unnecessary for me to quote examples.

But I must warn you that it is not easy to spot who is responsible for success or failure in the theatre, unless the play is so well known that its qualities can be taken for granted. A successful production is one in which there appears to be complete harmony between the play and the manner in which it has been staged. A lack of harmony can show itself in all sorts of ways. It may occur to you perhaps that the words which the actor is purring were meant to be the utterance of a violent and passionate man. The actor, as we say, is 'going against the text'. Or you may think that a play in which there has been a lot of insistence upon the poverty of the characters has been given a setting worthy of a flat in Mayfair; or that a woman who was clearly intended by the author to have an eye for fashionable clothes, appears in a succession of dowdy dresses and most immodish hats; and sometimes you will leave the theatre just feeling that something was not quite right, and you may try to get a printed copy of the play so that you can try to analyse just what was wrong.

This is an admirable practice but it is sometimes disappointing. When I saw Christopher Fry's difficult but moving play *A Sleep of Prisoners* on its first production I understood it sufficiently well to think that if I got hold of the book of the play and read it, I would be able to study each speech until I thoroughly understood it. I did but I didn't. I read it but I didn't understand it even as well as I had when seeing it performed; and I realized how exceptionally skilful the producer and actors had been. This sort of thing happens continually: lines that seem to be straightforward enough in reading suddenly reveal themselves as intensely telling, witty, moving, or even tragic, when brought to life on the stage by the actors. From simply reading *The School for Scandal* it's difficult to realize that the moment in the fourth act when the screen collapses and Lady Teazle is discovered behind it often makes audiences laugh for minutes on end. It's the same with Eliza Doolittle's 'Not bloody likely' in Bernard Shaw's *Pygmalion*, and John Worthing's entry clothed in black, mourning for a non-existent brother, in *The Importance of Being Earnest*: these moments are triumphs of the art of the dramatist.

But on other occasions you may read the text of a play after seeing it performed and realize that many fine passages or striking lines have been quite inadequately delivered. Jokes have fallen flat and characters have been misunderstood.

Everything to do with the theatre is active : acting, playing, seeing, doing, talking, even singing and dancing are all a part of the drama. The very word 'theatre' derives from a Greek word meaning 'a seeing-place' and 'drama' comes from another word meaning 'something that has been done'. In Greek times this something was an important religious ritual that was carried out in the spring and which had a kind of magical intention. So the very words *drama* and *theatre* signify the performance of something deeply significant—in a seeing-place occupied by members of the public.

The wretched dramatist finds then that he is collaborating not only with a company of actors and many other specialists but with the architect who designed the seeing-place or theatre and the audience which occupies it. I say 'wretched' because many talented writers who would like to write plays do find the complexity and hurly-burly of the theatre more than they can endure. A novelist needs a publisher and bookshops. A dramatist needs a company of actors sympathetic to his play, and a suitable theatre where it may be staged. That is to say that in the last resort a dramatist is absolutely dependent upon the skill and devotion of his actors and actresses and upon the critical appreciation of the public who have to be induced to leave their television sets and come to see his play in a theatre. This is why in the course of this book I shall constantly refer to the actors, the theatres (and their managers), and the audiences on whom even the greatest dramatists have been obliged to depend for their success. Now I want to describe what I mean by 'critical appreciation'.

2

No dramatist offers better opportunities for detective work in dramatic criticism than Shakespeare. We needn't stop to consider whether *Hamlet* is a great play or not. There are plenty of scholars who have pointed out its virtues and weaknesses. But it remains one of the most exciting and sheerly actable plays that has ever been written, and packed tight with dramatic poetry that has never been equalled in English and rarely in other languages. The character of the Prince has attracted most of the world's greatest actors. And what an astonishing number of different interpretations they have given of the role! Here let me beg my readers to beware of the person who on being asked what he thought of a certain performance replies, 'Oh it wasn't my idea of the part'. The aim of an actor, curiously enough, is not to give his, our friend's idea of the part, but his own. He will speak words and develop the actions and movements of the character as seem to be suggested by the play. He must convince the audience of the consistency of his interpretation. But the audience must be ready to be convinced—that is a part of the bargain. If you are only interested in one way of doing a part you had much better buy a gramophone record. Everyone who goes to the theatre is a dramatic critic; but criticism is not a matter of picking holes or of sitting back and waiting to be entertained and grumbling if you are not; or of hanging on to your own preferences and prejudices. The fun of dramatic criticism is in the attempt to understand, to perceive, what the dramatist is getting at, or what all those who have been concerned in the production think the dramatist is getting at. It is to appreciate the art of the actor who has to give an impression of being a credible living character even when he is speaking

sumptuous verse. It is nothing more than the faculty of sub-
mitting yourself to a story that is acted in front of you so
that you share the emotions of the characters and respond
to what they say.

But if you can't get to a theatre, go, as I say, to the
library. Most British plays, old as well as new, of any value
at all have been published (and so has plenty of junk) and
most of the classics are available in cheap well-printed
editions. The public library service is admirable. If you
can't find what you want on the shelves, ask one of the
librarians. Be persistent, and don't read difficult plays in
tattered, dusty, badly-printed editions that take the bloom
off Shakespeare himself. What other introductions to the
drama are there?

A play that has been filmed may turn out to be an
excellent film but it won't give you much idea of the
original play. The B.B.C. is continually giving us a chance
to hear the works of some of the outstanding British
dramatists. A broadcast performance of a play is a fine
test of some of its qualities, of its dialogue, the interest of
its subject, and in the most general way, what it is all about.
But the listener must still provide the visual side from his
mind's eye as much as if he were reading it to himself.

And don't forget how much pleasure and understanding
of a play can be got from reading it aloud, sitting round
the room with each part taken by a different person.

I must now bring one last matter to the notice of my
readers. There is a curious point about nearly all the plays
referred to in the first six chapters of this book and that is
that they are in verse. In fact, so far as I can discover, not
a single play was written in prose by the Greeks, the
Romans, or any other people who went in for writing plays

until the period that is known as the Renaissance. Plays
with dialogue in prose were written in Italy soon after the
year 1500. The first important play in English prose is Ben
Jonson's *Every Man in His Humour*, written in 1599. John
Lyly had used prose in the fifteen-eighties and I expect the
scholars will know of earlier examples. But for the most
part dramatists considered verse to be the proper medium
for drama. Verse, curiously, was a far more natural form
of speech and literature in olden times than it is today.

One of the most important qualities of a play is the
language in which it is written, and this quality of
language depends upon the quality of the spoken language
of the people. If therefore you find yourself complaining
at the difficulty of Shakespeare's language you must remember that the people of the first Elizabethan age spoke
a richer language than those of the second. Few people
write plays in verse today because so few of us read poetry
aloud or listen to others reading it. And nothing could be
less poetic than the vernacular that most of us speak today.
If we read too much we lose the use of our ears. In the
theatre we need all our faculties about us. Drama is something done and spoken, the more vividly the better.

SOME BOOKS FOR FURTHER READING :

It's well to remember that this book is about Drama, which
means plays, and not about the Theatre, which involves actors
and producers; otherwise I would start off by recommending
very strongly everything that has been written by Gordon
Craig. I do not know any other works of genius that discuss
the general principles of the drama and kindle a little flame

within each reader. Omniscient, panoramic, encyclopaedic kind of books like Allardyce Nicoll's *World Drama* and John Gastner's *Masters of the Drama* are so busy giving titles to hundreds of plays with snappy little judgments on most of them that the authors are short of wind for awakening enthusiasm and directing interest. There are two splendid books which will make you want to spend the rest of your life reading plays—William Archer's *Playmaking* and G. P. Baker's *Dramatic Technique*, neither as limited as the titles suggest. Both authors draw examples from the literature of the world, quoting particularly Shakespeare, Ibsen, Pinero, and Bernard Shaw.

C. E. Montague has an enthralling essay on The Literary Play in *A Writer's Notes on His Trade*, available as a Penguin. You may also find Geoffrey Crump's *Selections from English Dramatists* a useful book to read when you have finished the present one. It includes long extracts from many of the plays I have mentioned here.

Of course the best way to develop an interest in plays is to write one yourself.

CHAPTER TWO

The Anonymous Dramatists of the Middle Ages

THE STORY OF the British drama begins during the Middle Ages, a period of history remote from our own so far as drama goes. There were few books—which mattered little when there were few people who could read—and certainly no theatres. Yet in recent years we have begun to understand something of the real nature of medieval life and to perceive the misery and splendour, the violence and the charity, the poverty and wealth, the squalor and the luxury of those times, and to realize how fierce was the war between paganism and Christianity and how superlative were the achievements of men who had none of the technical resources of which we boast today but twice the passion.

I suppose that by standards of the twentieth century life in the Middle Ages was somewhat humdrum. Most people had to fall back on their own resources for entertainment and were all the richer for that; and the long cold winters must have seemed unbearably dreary. Yet there are many indications that medieval life was shot through with the most colourful and dramatic elements. The medieval nobility loved tournaments, the medieval middle-classes loved processions, the medieval churchmen loved festivals, and the remaining medieval people, the poor, the aged, the less well-paid workers, students and labourers, fell in with whatever was afoot, tournaments, processions, festivals, or any other kind of official high jinks, all of which were carried out with a high sense of what was intensely dramatic.

This is important to understand. A dramatic action is something done with purpose, with a sense of character and a sense of occasion. For example, there is nothing very dramatic about the May Day processions that take place in London on the Sunday nearest to May the first. A few thousand people with left-wing politics form up on the Embankment, march to Hyde Park, listen to speeches from their leaders, break up, and make their own way home. It would be very much more dramatic if the procession took place on May the first whatever day of the week it happened to be. It would be more dramatic still if some of the marchers were men who were striking over some particularly crucial political issue; and more so still if after the speeches they marched to the House of Commons and refused to leave the courtyard until they had been received by the Prime Minister; and if they were wearing clothes with some particular significance, the uniforms they had worn during the Great War, the working clothes they wear at the coal-face (if they were miners), or the white overalls that many decorators wear, the effect would be more dramatic still.

In a bustling medieval city like York there were frequent processions. Many of them were of a religious kind. They were a part of a great Church festival like Easter when many citizens of the town would fall in behind the clergy. Or they celebrated the feast day of a patron saint of one of the Guilds when all the masters, journeymen, and apprentices of the butchers, the bakers, the candlestick-makers, the shipwrights or the tailors would move in procession through the town from the head-quarters of their Guild to a chapel in the cathedral. They would be wearing their best clothes and carrying the emblems of their craft, designs embroidered on banners, or examples of their workmanship, and singing as they went. In the later Middle Ages, from perhaps the four-teenth century onwards, the finest processions were arranged when the king or some other very important personage visited the city. Then the streets were decorated, not in the rather haphazard fashion in which London was decorated for the Coronation of Queen Elizabeth II with twists of bunting and strings of flags and cardboard cut-out of the Royal Arms, but, if I may say so without offence, with far more style and purpose. The banners across the narrow streets would bear not the bleak word WELCOME but some telling Latin phrase, and from time to time the procession would stop before a small stage from which perhaps three attractive women representing the Graces would recite poems telling of the honour done to the city by the presence of the visitor. We have a number of examples of the kind of odes and poems that were recited on these occasions for they have been recorded by the late-medieval poet John Lydgate.

But perhaps the most memorable dramatic experience of all was provided by the churches and cathedrals. Between about 1050 and 1350 more than five thousand cathedrals, abbeys, and churches were built in Western Europe. This effort has been described as the greatest achievement ever accomplished by man except in time of war. It was the more remarkable in that anyone visiting

Europe around the year 700 A.D. might have been forgiven for thinking that nothing but disaster could overtake that continent of disordered, barbaric, savage, quarrelling, and disunited tribes. But a Christian historian writing about 1045 summarized what must have been the feelings of many people when he wrote that the world seemed to be 'doffing its old attire and putting on a new white robe of churches'.

And what churches they were! Is anyone so insensitive to wonder that he can take the cathedrals (so ridiculously called Gothic) for granted? How enormously impressive the great pile of Lincoln Cathedral must have been as the enormous structure rose upon the hill and dominated the whole landscape of the fens! And what must have been the feelings of the townsman as he paused before its great West Front and gazed at the sculptured stories from the Old Testament; or entering the tremendous nave, he saw on either side the glowing windows. Yet we have to go to a French cathedral like Chartres to learn properly about medieval iconography for here within and without there are close upon ten thousand figures representing almost the complete sum of Christian knowledge. In England such exquisite carvings proved to be admirable targets for the pikes and hatchets of the Puritans who with mistaken zeal destroyed the statues, smashed the stained-glass windows, and vandalized these shrines of medieval skill and idealism.

It's no use 'doing' a cathedral in a few minutes like a tourist. And although there's no need to go to the other extreme and develop a religious mysticism, one must be prepared to savour, to taste, to feel, to submit to the uniquely impressive atmosphere of these splendid buildings, and to realize the manner in which the medieval Church imposed upon the faithful and even, perhaps, the unbeliever, a sense of the majesty of God and the authority and splendour of His Church, through architecture, music, and ritual.

The ritual of the Catholic Church is still immensely impressive although it has been greatly modified since the time of its greatest splendour in the Middle Ages. Not even the most learned Catholic scholars know exactly how it was evolved; but starting off with the determination to celebrate and re-enact events in the life of Christ, the early fathers of the Church developed their ritual as a dramatist might do, by drawing material and looking for ideas from every possible source. It is really not surprising that in the middle of a group of rituals, divided among the various services of the Church—or Offices as they are called—someone should have stumbled upon the idea, almost by accident, of deliberate impersonation. The first tiny playlet, hardly identifiable as the beginning of the modern drama, depicted the arrival of the three Marys at the sepulchre where the body of the crucified Christ had been laid, to be told by the Angel of His resurrection. This beginning was made in a Swiss monastery. The idea caught on and over the years other experiments were made. As monks travelled from monastery to monastery they took their prompt-books with them. What had been done in the monastery of St Gallen in Switzerland was copied by a monastery in France on the banks of the Loire and then developed. The idea was passed on; and at a time when Latin was universally spoken and understood throughout Europe, a European drama was created. It was in Latin, it was sung, and the plays were always given in the churches. These plays, which eventually dramatized a number of episodes from the Bible and from the lives of the Saints, have come to be known as the 'liturgical drama', from the word for the Church's public services.

By 1300 or thereabouts many of these plays had become extremely elaborate, especially in France and England, and bishops welcomed them no longer within their cathedrals. Then the most remarkable thing happened. The less they were given in cathedrals, the more they were done in the market-places; the less by priests, the more by the people; the less in Latin, the more in vernacular languages.

In England this transformation, this liberation of the drama from the limitations of performance within a church, was closely associated with the Feast of Corpus Christi, a great religious mid-summer festival that was solemnized in the year 1310. The central feature of this festival was a procession through the town headed by the Bishop and his clergy and followed by the people who marched not individually but in their Crafts, Guilds, Confraternities, or whatever societies or associations they were members of. They sang as they processed and at certain places they stopped, the Bishop offered up prayers, and then they sang another hymn. There can be little doubt that at these stopping-places there were erected small stages or platforms; on them stood a person representing or impersonating a figure from history, in this case from Church history. And I have no doubt that these ' impersonators ' were given something to say as would have happened if it had been a Prince making an ' Entry '. But in this case the words would not have been an ode of welcome, but a quotation from the Bible perhaps.

Now the protagonist was not a Prince but the people,

whether they were taking part in the procession or watching it. And since all the people must have wanted to see all the stages it probably occurred to the authorities that it would be easier to bring the stages to the people, by making a procession of them, than the people to the stages as happens in modern theatres. So Church and Town authorities laid their heads together and created a religious drama that took place in the streets of their city.

There exist five groups of plays that are known as *Corpus Christi plays*. They were given on the day of the feast or on the next or following days. The collection of plays that comes from York originally numbered more than fifty short plays and these were distributed among the Guilds of the city, each Guild taking one play. The Guild then equipped itself with a kind of stage on wheels —we know very little about the design—which was called a 'Pageant'. This vehicle was hauled through the town by a group of men, not by horses, and at a dozen or so places where a crowd of citizens had collected it stopped and the play was given. So the Guild that was giving the first play in the collection, or cycle, headed the procession of pageants, and was followed by the rest. What a splendidly colourful commotion there must have been in a city where such performances were given!

Although we know a certain number of details about the manner in which these plays were originally performed— details of the costumes that were worn and of the payments made to the actors—there are still many points we do not understand, particularly how it came about that the plays were given in this curious processional manner. We can guess but we have no definite knowledge. I would simply say this : their performance gives a vivid impression of three things—civic pride, religious devotion, and enormous pleasure in the work.

Now let me say a few words about the plays themselves. In general they follow a similar pattern. The cycles usually begin with a play which shows God creating the world. It is followed by a play depicting the fall of Lucifer, then by the Garden of Eden and the episode of the Fall of Man. Most cycles include a play about Noah but little else from the Old Testament. Christ's Nativity is usually dealt with at considerable length but there is little from His ministry. Passion week is depicted in the fullest detail. The Crucifixion is usually followed by plays showing the Resurrection, the Last Judgment, and other subjects of which I shall say more in a moment. They deal in short with the Christian message in fullest detail; their scope is nothing less than the whole story of the fall, the redemption, and the resurrection of man.

The oldest cycle comes not from one of the wealthy English cities but from the Keltic stronghold of Cornwall. I do not propose to say much about these plays for they are written in an ancient Cornish dialect and no adequate translation into English has been published. The plays are divided into three groups for performance on consecutive days, the Creation of the World, the Passion of Our Lord, and the events following the Crucifixion. Unhappily we do not know where these plays were performed or under what circumstances. They do not appear to have been *Corpus Christi plays*.

As to the English cycles, their authorship is as much a mystery as a good many other things about them. The Chester cycle appears to have been the work of a single dramatist. The other cycles have been developed by as many as three different poets writing at different times, each taking the work of his predecessor, developing and adding to it, giving in some cases variety of style and treatment to the whole. Some towns, not very surprisingly, seem to have been unable to discover a particularly gifted writer and so borrowed the manuscript of a neighbouring and more fortunate town, made their own copy, and added perhaps a play or two of their own.

The oldest surviving manuscript in English comes from Chester. It consists of twenty-five plays which seem to have been the work of one man. The York cycle consists of forty-eight plays and at one time probably included at least three more. This great body of plays is the work of at least three gifted dramatists. The third cycle is sometimes known as the Towneley cycle from the name of the man who for many years owned the manuscript. There are thirty-two plays, many of which are similar to those in the York cycle, and it is thought to have been played in Wakefield. The fourth surviving cycle comes from Coventry. Only two plays of the original ten survive. The first of the two, the famous *Pageant of the Shearmen and Taylors* is an exquisite telling of the story of the Nativity, a masterpiece of medieval dramatic literature. The fifth and last surviving cycle has the unfortunate name of the *Hegge* manuscript or the *Ludus Coventriae*. It is even known as the *North Towne play*. Scholars have now established, I think, that these plays have nothing to do with Coventry but were most likely to have been written at Lincoln and performed outside its great cathedral. It consists of forty-two plays which were clearly written to be staged on a fixed platform as was usually the way in France and not on movable pageants.

I cannot pretend that even the five English cycles are easy to read. Complete versions have only been published in the original middle English and the single plays, of which there are a number of collections, do not give any idea of the superb scope of the full cycles. Performances of the *Corpus Christi plays* have to be thought of in terms not of hours but of days. The plays are immense, sprawling, timeless. They are of another world from the play that can be visited between supper and the last train home. We know that the first play was usually given soon after daybreak and one imagines that the cheerful citizens of the town devoted the rest of the day and as many more days as necessary to watching these great pageants trundle up to unfold another episode in the tremendous story of God and Man. And indeed, as I have already suggested, what a rumbling there must have been as the carts banged along over cobble-stoned streets, the actors prepared for performance, the audience strained and chattered with excitement, discussing what they had just seen and anticipating the next. In France where these cycles were usually given on fixed stages, some are known to have lasted forty days!

What I want to urge is the splendour of their conception, for the most wonderful thing about them—and I use the word 'wonderful' deliberately—is quite simply the fact that the people of medieval England conceived, wrote, staged, acted, and watched a succession of plays that told the finest story known to man. It is only a little less remarkable that they are written in an English which rolls splendidly off the tongue and in rhythms that beat incessantly and gloriously in the head. Yet a celebrated critic of English literature can write 'From the literary point of view the workmanship [of these plays] is never far from crude and, in the older strata, insipid to a degree'.

And so the cycles open with God upon his throne, raised above the level of the other actors even though they were on a cart. He had a purple robe, a golden face, and prolific beard. Here are the splendid lines with which the York plays begin. They are slightly modernized.

> *I am gracious and great, God without a beginning,*
> *I am maker unmade, all might is in me.*
> *I am life and way unto wealth winning* [wealth is health]
> *I am foremost and first, as I bid it shall be.*

God announces that he has created the world and man to live upon it. The angels praise his achievement. Then we are shown the proud, overweening Lucifer:

> *O! What I am nimble and fair and figured full fit!*
> *The form of all fairness upon me lies fast;*
> *All wealth in my wield is, I know by my wit,*
> *The beams of my brightness are built with the best.*

God strikes and Lucifer and his minions plunge to Hell. We are usually shown the full episode of man's disobedience in the Garden of Eden with Eve clothed in 'white hosen' and a 'hair' or wig, and the serpent with a tail. Satan tempts Eve with the charming lines:

> *Bite on boldly, be nought abashed,*
> *And bear some to Adam to amend his mood*
> *And also his bliss.*

And Eve passes the apple to Adam with the words:

I
*The Play of the
Exodus*
York, 1957

II   The Dance of Death   III   Death in *Everyman*

IV   Another version of *Everyman*

Bite on boldly for it is true,
We shall be gods and know all thing.

One of the favourite subjects of these dramatists was the story of Noah and the flood, an exquisite version of which is to be found in the Chester cycle. It is rightly included in most collections of these plays for it is very amusing, very moving, and very actable. Its charm lies not so much in the verse which flows gently along to a consistent rhythmic pattern as in its deep humanity and humour. How the dramatist must have chortled as he wrote the part of Noah's wife who doesn't want to go on board her husband's ship but would rather stay on dry land and drink Malmsey wine with her gossips!

There is one striking play about Cain and Abel included in the Wakefield cycle, but on the whole the dramatists had little interest in the Old Testament apart from the prophets who foretold the coming of the Son of God.

The Nativity scenes are usually marked with a great tenderness. The fullest version of the story comes from Coventry. This famous and exquisite play includes a Herod, who according to one of the few stage directions, 'rages both on the pageant and also in the street' creating alarm and excitement and I daresay a good deal of amusement among the crowded spectators. The slaughter of the children at the command of Herod is immediately followed by the singing of the lovely carol 'Lullay, lullay, thou little tiny child', which in the fifteenth century must have been sung by choirboys.

It is among the Nativity plays that we come across the work of a man of outstanding literary skill. The Wakefield cycle contains six plays, on Cain, on Noah, two plays about

3

the shepherds, and plays about the buffeting and scourging of Christ on the way to the Crucifixion, which are clearly the work of a man of outstanding literary skill, with a strong sardonic sense of humour, and a bitter resentment against social injustice. This dramatist has come to be known as the Wakefield Master. His two plays on the shepherds are full of striking dramatic effects. Indeed the *Wakefield Second Shepherds Play*, as it is usually called, is often given as a one-act play; for it departs from the Bible story to develop an episode in which a rogue called Mac hypnotizes the shepherds into a deep sleep and then steals one of their sheep. When they wake and find what has happened they go to his cottage and find the sheep in a child's cot with Mac's wife crooning lullabies to it. As punishment they toss the sheep-stealer in a blanket. Here the dramatist creates a powerful stage-effect by following the horse-play of the blanket-tossing episode with the appearance of the Angel announcing the birth of Christ.

The most fully developed group of plays is usually that which tells the story of the Passion. The group included in the Lincoln cycle is particularly impressive, employing what is now called a multiple setting. The dramatist shows the tumultuous events of Holy Week by means of action moving quickly from stage to stage. On one we have Christ and his disciples, on another the elders of the Jews, on another Pilate, and the crowds that must have thronged the streets of Jerusalem, now calling to Christ as he rode through the streets of the city on a donkey, now calling for his death in front of the Sanhedrin.

Of quite a different kind is the Passion sequence from the York cycle. Each separate episode, the entry of Jesus into Jerusalem, the Last Supper, the Agony in the Garden, and the betrayal of Judas is shown at length. The dramatist depicts the grimly humorous brutality of the soldiers set to guard Jesus and erect the cross to which he had already been nailed. He depicts Pilate as an elegant nobleman, who on his first appearance is making love to his wife, while his Beadle, a comic character, wants to talk business. When Lady Procula is finally packed off to bed, Pilate lies down with the words:

Pilate: *I command thee to come near, for I will go to my couch,*
          Hold in thy hands tenderly and heave me behind,
          And look that thou tease me not with thy tasting,
          but tenderly me touch.
Beadle: *Ah, sir, ye weigh well!*
Pilate: *Yea, I have wet me with wine.*
          Yet hold me down and lap me even here,
          For I will slyly sleep unto sin.
          Look that no man nor no minion of mine
          With no noise be nighing me near.

But neither Pilate nor his wife are to have a quiet night. Lady Procula has a dream in which Satan rages against Jesus and Pilate is woken by Annas and Caiaphas bringing Jesus in front of him 'to answer his crimes'. The trials and examinations that follow are passages of sustained and powerful writing in which many kinds of dramatic effect are used with the greatest skill.

The scenes of the Crucifixion do not end the cycle. Death, in Christian theology, is not the end of man. That was the supreme message of Jesus Christ. Jesus died that men might believe in the resurrection of the body. Accordingly the York cycle has no less than twelve plays following the Crucifixion, dealing with the Harrowing of Hell, the

Resurrection of Jesus, the incredulity of (doubting) Thomas, the Ascension, the death of Mary, the Assumption of the Virgin, and the Last Judgment, while the Chester cycle includes a tremendous play on Antichrist.

Are they not magnificently dramatic subjects? Let me remind you that the famous medieval legend of the Harrowing of Hell describes the visit of Jesus to the Underworld. He beats on the gates demanding that they be opened—he is given ringing Latin sentences—sweeps through Hell to the consternation of the devils, and liberates Adam and the Prophets who have been languishing in the deepest gloom for upwards of four thousand years.

To us these plays are full of the greatest dramatic interest. If we are Christians they have considerable theological interest besides. But how intensely thrilling they must have been to medieval audiences for whom the existence of Hell, ruled over by Lucifer, was a terrifying reality. I think that we can only hope to understand the medieval world by remembering that the Gothic cathedrals were not museums around which tourists traipsed as they do today even during services; that the *Corpus Christi plays* were not an excessively wordy but rather colourful collection of plays too difficult to stage and poorly written compared with *Hamlet* and *King Lear*; that Hell was not a picturesque idea and Heaven a colloquialism for a good time: cathedrals and plays and Heaven and Hell, the wrath of God and eternal life, were the impressive realities of medieval life. The plays were written and acted as an act of faith, not to entertain people too tired or lazy to entertain themselves.

I wonder constantly who they were, these anonymous

dramatists of such skill and passion. They may have been monks, men who passed their lives in a monastery dedicated to some literary or artistic task or even in perpetual meditation. They may have been clerics, men trained in the schools attached to the monasteries and cathedrals but who earned their living in some secular employment. They may have been unfrocked monks, like some of the men who wrote the finest medieval poetry, men who were filled with the splendour of God's word but who were unable to submit to the intense discipline of monastic life and to resist the clamour of a city square on market-day. Or they may have been minstrels. Have you come across the medieval legend, charmingly recounted by Anatole France, of the minstrel who stood before an altar in a church and went through his tricks in honour of the Virgin Mary and was saved from expulsion by the furious monks by the miraculous appearance of the Virgin herself? For though we usually consider minstrels to have been colourful but disreputable figures entertaining crowds with performing monkeys or by singing lewd songs or with juggling and acrobatics, it was the minstrels who composed and sang some of the finest songs of the Middle Ages, and not only songs but wondrous epic poems of many thousand lines.

But whoever they were, they must have been learned men, for it is thought that they took many an idea from the French who in these matters moved more quickly than the English. They were also familiar with the literature of the time. As you will have noticed, they did not take all their subjects from the Bible which was treated then with less respect than it has been in more recent times, and was far less well known, but from the works of early Christian writers, which, though excellent to read, were not considered good enough to be included in the Bible, as well as from religious books of their own time.

And now, you may ask, if these plays are as fine as all that, why are they not more popular today? The answer to this is that their qualities are not the qualities we now admire in literature and drama. I have spoken of the timelessness of the *Corpus Christi plays*. Time is precious to modern men. We have a sickening expression 'time is money'. Ough! We like to get to the point of something quickly, we value a sense of economy and intensity. It's only a crank who would go to Paris by riding on horseback and crossing the Channel in a sailing ship when a dozen different airlines are at his disposal. Yet will not the crank be richer perhaps in human experience?

The people of the Middle Ages were far more familiar with death than we are today. But did not this ensure that in some ways they valued life the more highly?

SOME BOOKS FOR FURTHER READING:

It is shocking that the great English cycles of *Corpus Christi plays* should not be readily available in a complete and scholarly edition and in a tactful translation for the general reader. The excellent editions of the Early English Text Society are difficult to obtain and no easy reading for those unfamiliar with Middle English. An exception must be made of *The York Cycle of Miracle Plays*, edited and (slightly) modernized by the Rev. J. S. Purvis.

There are various collections of which the following are the most readily available:

Everyman and Medieval Miracle Plays edited by A. C. Cawley in the Everyman Library (1956 edition) gives fourteen well-edited plays selected from the existing cycles to give a concept of their scope.

Three Medieval Plays edited, and in the case of the French *Pierre Pathelin* translated, by John Allen, includes the splendid *Coventry Nativity Play*. This is published by Heinemann.

Most libraries contain other selections.

The standard books on the medieval drama are: E. K. Chambers's *The Medieval Stage,* and more recent, Hardin Craig's *English Medieval Drama.* Both are long and learned.

The first volume of the *Penguin Guide to English Literature* is full of helpful information about medieval life, thought and literature, and prints two plays. J. Huizinga's *The Waning of the Middle Ages,* also available as a Penguin, gives a splendid picture of the dramatic quality of the Middle Ages in its declining years.

And here I feel I ought to add a note explaining two terms which constantly crop up in connection with the Medieval drama. The words 'Mystery plays' and 'Miracle plays' are used rather indiscriminately. The term Miracle play is fairly straightforward for it refers to plays which dealt with the lives of the Saints and particularly of the Virgin Mary and of the miracles they achieved.

Mystery play is said to refer to the Guilds who acted the plays and who often called their craft a 'mystery'. This explanation is not altogether satisfactory, because the word was used in France in its modern sense, denoting something secret which may only be revealed in special circumstances.

For ordinary purposes it can be taken that both terms refer to the religious drama of the Middle Ages.

CHAPTER THREE

The Author of *Everyman*

THIS CHAPTER IS about three dramatists. Two of them lived and wrote during the fifteenth century, when the dramatists I spoke about in the last chapter were putting the final touches to the Corpus Christi cycles. The third probably lived in the early sixteenth century.

One thing of which we can be fairly certain is that most medieval dramatists owed a very great deal to the French. They were the dramatic innovators of the Middle Ages. But having said that I must remind you that from the time of William the Conqueror until the final defeat of the English at the end of the Hundred Years War, England and France were in many ways a single country. The English kings ruled over large parts of France. Medieval French was spoken on both sides of the Channel and medieval Latin was spoken throughout Western Europe. So that in some ways educated people in the two countries had a better idea of what the other crowd were doing than we have today and there was a very considerable interchange of manuscripts, of ideas, and of experiences between men of similar interests.

Yes, the French were certainly the most enterprising people in Europe in the composition of plays. In 1285 a minstrel of Arras called Adam le Bossu wrote a play of a kind that was not attempted in England for more than two hundred years. Long before the liturgical dramas had become unpopular in churches the French had begun to write plays full of religious significance but on secular subjects, in French instead of Latin, and to be performed anywhere but in a church. The English followed suit, although with a good deal less skill and enthusiasm.

On the other hand, I don't want to suggest that the English medieval dramatists did little but imitate the French. Their invention was perhaps a little more sluggish but the French did not produce a single poet to compare with Geoffrey Chaucer. And even when the English did follow a French example they transformed the work to make it thoroughly their own and wholly English.

By 1350, when the Hundred Years War was well under way and flowing strongly in favour of England, drama of one kind or another, in Latin and in the vernacular, performed in churches and without, on religious and to a lesser extent on secular subjects, was firmly established in both countries. And it is understandable, I think, that the men who were possessed with enthusiasm for writing in dramatic form, should have begun to feel their way towards other subjects than those involved in the composition of a *Corpus Christi play*.

That these subjects should have remained religious is understandable since the only available education in England was a religious one. But a Christian outlook on life did not limit a man's interests to the stories in the Bible. If you study the statues in a Gothic cathedral—and I repeat that this is more easily done in France than England —you will usually find not only kings and prophets and bishops, angels and devils, and scores of other historical and mythological personages, but certain abstract characters such as the Three Graces. You must remember that the Christian Church has never won its fight for the Kingdom of God and the soul of man, and during the Middle Ages it had to fight for its very existence. It lost no chance to assert its authority and describe its message; and how could that message be better presented than superbly drawn and coloured in a stained-glass window, acted in a vivid play, or celebrated in a piece of glorious music that sent the heavenly voices wonderfully echoing among the transepts of a Gothic church. The Church's message was that man must win a place for himself in Paradise and eternal bliss by the quality of the life he leads on earth. Isn't it a great deal more telling to assert that a man must go through life holding Virtue by one hand and Knowledge by the other, and that whenever he meets Desire or Greed or Anger he must cross to the other side of the road, than simply to warn him to be a good fellow and avoid getting into trouble? And isn't it more impressive still if he passes into a church, where he is going to confess his sins and celebrate his communion with Jesus Christ, between exquisite stone figures of Virtue and Charity and misshapen deformed effigies of the Seven Deadly Sins?

This kind of art is known as allegory. It was almost the universal custom among medieval writers and artists to work allegorically, presenting abstract ideas in concrete fashion. But unfortunately allegory has become so closely identified with preachiness that we have little use for it in the twentieth century. As soon as we suspect that a dramatist has intended a certain character to be a symbol of something or other we're inclined to feel we're being got at, throw up a barrier of resentment, and go into our shell. And in defence of such a reaction I must say that the fault is as much with the dramatists as with their audiences. For as soon as a modern dramatist becomes more interested in a type than in a particular character, the life seems to depart from him and his work, and leaves a dismal parody of a living man.

But the loss is ours, for the scope of our drama is lessened. Listen to the theme of one of the earliest plays to have survived that has nothing to do with the liturgical drama or with the Feast of Corpus Christi. It was found in a chest full of old papers in a Dublin priory, written on the back of some accounts—though perhaps the accounts were written on the back of it. It has no title. The man who first edited it called it *The Pride of Life*. It seems to have been written around the year 1410. Large parts of the dialogue are missing. The story, so far as it can be reconstructed, describes how the King of Life sends a challenge to Death to come and fight with him. He packs off the Bishop who comes to intercede and awaits the duel. In fight the King is worsted and goes to Hell; but he is redeemed and brought back to earth by the intercession of his Queen.

At this point I would like to throw a rather personal challenge at the heads of my readers. The idea of a man in the power of his health and strength challenging Death to a duel is one that has enthralled man for many thousands of years and formed the subject of a good many incidents both in literature and mythology. If you do not thrill at the idea of such an encounter, of yourself writing such a duologue, or of seeing what other men may have made of it, our ideas of what is dramatic are very different, for I can think of nothing that stirs me more intensely.

One cannot say very much about such a mangled text

as that of *The Pride of Life*; but it was not many years
later that a dramatist of something approaching genius
wrote a 'morality', as these plays are called, that is among
the masterpieces of medieval art. The play is called *The
Castle of Perseverance*. This time it is the author's own
title. The theme of the play is nothing less than the life
of Man from the cradle to the grave. His canvas, you see,
was only a trifle smaller than that of the dramatists of the
Corpus Christi plays.

By the greatest of good fortune a plan for the staging
of the play is attached to the manuscript. This plan shows
a circular arrangement of scaffolds or stages, each representing a different scene, with the castle in the middle.
The spectators presumably sat or stood all the way round
the setting which must have been rather like a circus arena
with a large construction built of wood in the middle.

By means of these different stages the dramatist gave
himself a good deal of scope; and it must have been
immensely impressive as the various characters introduced
themselves, each from his own stage, the World, Belial,
and Flesh, each using words that certainly are not lacking
in power. Here for example are the opening words of
Belial :

Now I sit, Satanas, in my sad sin,
As devil doughty, in draf as a drake.
I champ and I chase, I choke on my chin,
I am boist'rous and bold, as Belial the blake.
What folk that I grope, their gaping and grenne.
I wis from Carlisle into Kent my carping they take.
Both the back and the buttock bursteth all on brenne [fire].

Here I should add that a delightful direction written

upon the plan of the scene directs that 'he that shall play
Belial, look that he have gun-powder burning in pipes in
his hands and in his ears when he goeth into battle'. This
surely called for heroism on the part of the actor, but the
effect must have been tremendous. It is then announced that
Man has been born and he is led into the world by two
Angels, a good and a bad. Like many another since, this
man finds the promises of worldly pleasure made him by
the Bad Angel far more attractive than the life of abstin-
ence which is demanded by the Good Angel. He is led to
the stage of the World where he is quickly surrounded
by Lust, Folly, and all the Seven Deadly Sins gorgeously
attired. There is a long powerful and savage scene in
which the Seven Deadly Sins try to win Man for Hell,
but eventually the Virtues are successful in turning him
from his evil ways, and to protect him from himself they
immure him in the Castle of Perseverence where they are
beseiged by the Seven Sins. In a most skilful manner the
dramatist now develops a long and violent scene in which
the World and its Evils fight among themselves, as much
at loggerheads with each other as with Mankind, using
as their Messenger a macabre character called Backbiter
who announces that he is 'a mad messenger leaping
throughout the world, far and near, unsaid sayings to say'.
Eventually Belial leads the assault upon the castle, but the
Virtues beat back the enemy by bombarding them with—
roses! (The rose, during the Middle Ages, seems to have
been a kind of symbol both of the enchantment of the
worldly life and the purity of the religious. While the
feature of many of the French cathedrals is a rose window
—a triumph of artistic design and execution—the rose is
sometimes shown as the symbol of something that man

will go through the fire of Hell itself to pick.) But the dramatist was not a sentimentalist. It is Avarice who finally lures Man into surrender and it is a very moving scene when this evil figure advances alone upon the castle and leads Man away from the Virtues back to his former evil life. He is then struck down by Death; and lest the audience should be in any doubt about the meaning of the play, it ends with the four Daughters of God contending for Man's soul, debating his worth, setting his virtues against his vices, but leaving the last word to God himself.

A number of other moralities survive and have received a good deal less than their due in the history books. The trouble is that nobody wants them. In literature they are overshadowed by Chaucer while their theatrical qualities are difficult to assess. This is understandable because they are nowadays rarely performed and if it is difficult to judge a modern play by reading it, it is a great deal worse with a morality of the fifteenth century. Yet although they are enormously important in the history of the drama they are surely worth reading and performing for their own sake. Their moral quality gives them a seriousness and a purpose which we banish from the theatre at the risk of triviality. Their authors are preoccupied with the great moral issues of life, the nature of sin, and the difficulty of living a decent life in the middle of so many so highly attractive worldly pleasures. They are sometimes lit with passages of great lyrical beauty and *Hickscorner,* a play that growls to be performed, has a lurid scowling quality that reminds one of the Wakefield Master though without his humour.

What kind of men were the authors of these plays?

Minstrels or monks? They were less constrained by the need for religious conformity even than the Wakefield Master. They were a good deal more conscious of the need to entertain their audiences. In fact there are indications that for the first time in British history they were writing for men who earned their living by acting their plays.

Not so the author of *Everyman*. *Everyman* is generally agreed to have been taken from a Flemish original. This play was the work of a monk called Petrus, or Peter, from the town of Diest, but the English translator has done his work with such consummate skill that the Flemish, I am sure, will forgive the inclusion of this play in a book on the work of British dramatists.

The subject of *Everyman* is not unlike that of *The Pride of Life*. The difference is that in this case we are dealing not with a King but with every man, with anyone; and he is not so aglow in his health and supreme in confidence that he can challenge Death to a duel : Death summons him, as Death so often summons the best of us, when we are least prepared; he is not reprieved from the grave : the whole play describes his attempts to prepare himself for death.

Those who make high claims for the theatre, believing it to be a place where the great issues of life and death should be presented and discussed, will find all the seriousness of intention they want in *Everyman*. Those who value their time so highly that they like their drama to be highly concentrated will find the sixty-five minutes of *Everyman* as stripped of amiable digressions as anyone could wish.

Everyman begins at the moment when most moralities finish, when a Man in the full bloom of life senses the terrifying fingers of Death at his heart. God, who laments the behaviour of the people for whom his Son died, summons Death his 'mighty messenger'.

Death: *Almighty God I am here at your will*
        Your commandment to fulfil.
God: *Go thou to Everyman*
        And shew him, in my name,
        A pilgrimage he must on him take
        Which he in no wise may escape;
        And he bring with him a sure reckoning
        Without delay or any tarrying.
Death: *Lord, I will in the world go run over all*
        And cruelly outsearch both great and small.
        He that loveth riches I will strike with my dart
        His sight to blind, and from Heaven to depart—
        Except that alms be his good friend—
        In Hell for to dwell, world without end.
        Yonder I see Everyman walking . . .
        His mind is on fleshly lusts and his treasure . . .

He assails Everyman. Everyman falters, wriggles, complains, argues, pleads. Death will allow him no respite. Everyman must make himself ready to present a reckoning of his life before 'God in his magnificence'. Everyman, unable to bear the thought of the ghastly loneliness of Death, thinks of his drinking companion, Fellowship. Why, of course, he'll do anything reasonable to help Everyman, even to committing murder . . . but to die for him, that is asking too much of a friend. Everyman thinks of his relatives. They flatly refuse. Cannot his wealth help him? Cannot he buy his way out of trouble?

    Alas I have thee loved and had great pleasure
    All my life days on goods and treasure

he says to his Goods; but the answer is sharp:

V   An open-air stage in Holland

VI   Dancing in the 16th century

VII   A spectacle from Renaissance Italy

That is to thy damnation without lying.
For my love is contrary to the love everlasting.

Has he done no good deeds that he might summon to
his aid? His Good Deeds are in poor condition. They have
nothing to say on his behalf. They are lying 'cold in
ground'. He helps her to her feet and asks her advice. She
advises him to summon Knowledge. Knowledge enters
with the lovely couplet:

Everyman, I will go with thee and be thy guide
In thy most need to go by thy side.

Now he is in better fettle and with Good Deeds and
Knowledge on each side of him he thinks of the Church,
goes to Confession, and does penance with a scourge. This
part of the play is intensely Catholic; but the skill with
which the dramatist has handled this difficult theme makes
the play far greater than a piece of religious propaganda.
And he achieves this development by means of his allegory.
The dramatic structure of the play is astonishingly powerful. Everyman in panic at the imminence of Death turns
to friends and relatives and to his wealth. They let him
down. He tries to justify himself on a higher plane, trying
to recall what good deeds he may have done and what
knowledge he may have acquired. He seeks the help of the
Church, and having been put into a state of grace and
worthy to meet his God, he summons in one last act of
confidence his faculties, Discretion, Strength, Five Wits,
and Beauty. Together they make a pilgrimage to the very
mouth of the grave. But a man does not die with his
faculties about him. Therein lies the loneliness of death,
and its horror if you are hounded into the grave by guilt.

4

In turn his faculties desert him. Even Knowledge is of no avail in the last resort and Good Deeds alone goes with him into the earth.

That the author of *Everyman* was a priest there can be very little doubt. He clearly was not interested in fine language for its own sake, he had no use for 'effective' situations, striking scenic effects, comic characters, or any of the other diversions that delight us in the *Corpus Christi plays* and the Moralities. He has written a triumphantly successful play because he knew, understood, and was deeply sympathetic towards human beings, because he knew, understood, and had deep faith in the Catholic Church; and because he had the gift of writing from the heart, straightforwardly, unselfconsciously, his language exactly suited to his thoughts, his feelings, and his dramatic purpose.

Everyman, I would say, is unique in the dramatic literature of the world in being a play on a subject of supreme and universal interest, told with a sharp clear mastery of dramatic art. It is a moral play and it achieves its purpose by the use of allegory. Must one not deeply respect an age that can give birth to a drama of this kind? Have we the least right to dismiss *Everyman* from a discussion of dramatic art because it has a profoundly religious purpose? Can the drama serve a higher function than to present before its audiences the great issues of life and death? And is not our theatre the poorer for its divorce from things that matter?

I put these ideas as questions because I do not want to be dogmatic about this important subject. One is only entitled to lay down the law about trivialities. I shall return to it in my final chapter.

SOME BOOKS FOR FURTHER READING :

It is symptomatic of the present attitude towards the
Morality plays that there does not exist a single published
book which discusses them in a scholarly and sympathetic
fashion, as interesting plays and not as unsuccessful pieces of
literature except A. P. Rossiter's facetiously written *English
Drama.*

Texts are also scarce. No moralities are included in any of
the cheap editions of the English classics except *Everyman*
itself which appears in the book of that name in the Everyman Library. *Everyman* also appears in John Allen's *Three
Medieval Plays.* Four moralities are printed in hideous
double columns in J. Quincey Adams *Chief Pre-Shakespearian Dramas* (along with many other most interesting and
inaccessible plays), but it is out of print. J. M. Manley's
Specimens of the Pre-Shakespearian Drama is finely printed
but difficult to obtain. Another important morality, though
later and far more theatrically elaborate than those I have
been discussing, Sir David Lindsay's *A Satire of the Three
Estates,* has been published by Heinemann in the shortened
version of Robert Kemp which has had considerable success
at the Edinburgh Festival.

CHAPTER FOUR

Christopher Marlowe

THERE WERE VERY roughly fifty years between the composition of *Everyman* and the birth of Christopher Marlowe. During this half century the drama, as we know it today, was created. This is a very simple thing to say and a very considerable thing really to appreciate. The *Corpus Christi plays* and the moralities have almost nothing in common with the sort of plays we expect to see in theatres of our own time. But Marlowe's plays are not only recognizable: they are often revived. In addition to this they are reasonably easy to understand and immensely exciting to read.

The extraordinary thing about the creation of the drama was that it was very largely the work of amateurs. All sorts of people had a hand in it: schoolmasters for instance: a Nicolas Udall wrote a famous play called *Ralph Roister Doister*; and bishops: an Irish bishop called John Bale wrote an extraordinary historical play called *King John,* and the Bishop of Bath and Wells, John Still, wrote a lusty and improper comedy called *Gammer Gurton's Needle*; two young lawyers, Thomas Norton and Thomas Sackville wrote the first English tragedy, *Gorboduc*; and it is clear from the number of Elizabethan writers who were educated at Cambridge that there was considerable interest in the drama at the Universities. And then there were the first professional dramatists and entertainers such as the famous John Heywood who married the daughter of Sir John More, himself a notable scholar and nobleman and a great patron of the drama.

When we find that during a certain period a number of interesting plays have been written, we can be reasonably sure that there also existed actors to act them; and actors nearly always band themselves together into companies. Some of the Moralities which I mentioned in the last chapter were clearly written to be acted by small companies of actors, early professionals in fact. For instance there is in one play a break in the middle just before the first impressive appearance of that most entertaining character, the Devil, so that a collection could be taken.

By the time of the Tudor kings, Henry VII and Henry VIII, it had become fashionable throughout Europe for kings and noblemen to support, at least for certain parts of the year, small companies of actors, singers and entertainers, to amuse the members of their court, their household, or their guests, in the long winter evenings, and to supply the entertainment on festive occasions. When these small companies were not being employed by their noble lord they used to go on tour and give performances where we would expect to find the biggest gathering of people wanting amusement, namely in the inns, taverns, and hostelries of the market-towns. They set up improvised stages in inn-yards and played to a public standing around the stage or sitting on improvised trestles. There were at least four hostelries in London where performances of this kind were given.

Then in 1576 there took place an event of tremendous

importance for the theatre. A certain James Burbage, who at this time was a little over forty years old, a joiner by trade and an actor in the company attached to the Earl of Leicester, borrowed some money from his brother-in-law, who was a grocer, and built a theatre. He built it in Shoreditch, just outside the precincts of the city of London, and he called it The Theatre. Of the design of this building we know absolutely nothing at all. People guess that it must have had a large stage surrounded by a space where people stood as in the inn-yards, enclosed perhaps by a gallery or two, though whether the whole was round or square we have no idea. But it was clearly thought to have been a good idea, for James Burbage was flattered by the erection of a second theatre, very close to The Theatre, and this was called The Curtain. These two theatres served the city of London for twenty years. They were of the utmost importance in the early life of Christopher Marlowe.

Christopher Marlowe was born in Canterbury in 1564. He did tolerably well at the Canterbury Grammar School and won a scholarship to Cambridge where there was a great and growing interest in the drama. Marlowe was intended to be a priest. His education therefore involved a considerable amount of Latin, Greek, and rhetoric. The study of the classics, which instead of killing his interest awoke his enthusiasm, can be seen in the tremendous number of classical references that crop up throughout his plays. The study of rhetoric might be described as exercises in improvised speaking. The ideal was to think clearly and express those thoughts in the clearest and most effective manner possible, not only in the choice of words but in the diction and tone with which they were delivered and with the appropriate gestures—a very proper training for a priest; and also, as it seems to me, a very excellent one for a dramatist.

Marlowe, while at Cambridge, had aroused in him all the passions of his life, the classics, the drama, and the power of words. It is impossible to read a few pages of any play by Marlowe without sensing the delight he must have had in the act of composition.

His first literary work that we know anything about was not a play but a translation. Consistently with the kind of young man he seems to have been he chose to translate a work by one of the most passionate and sensual of Roman poets—Ovid. His second work was a play. The subject, *Dido, Queen of Carthage,* was both passionate and sensual. It was at once performed, as far as we know in Cambridge, which is not surprising for although it is an undeveloped piece of work it has a splendour of language that was new to English ears. He wrote a second play and seems to have placed it with one of the two London companies before he had even left Cambridge. This is astonishing : but then everything about Marlowe is astonishing. He was at Cambridge to become a priest; but one of the few things we know about him for certain is that he became an atheist. Since he took his M.A. in 1587 at the age of twenty-three he must have worked hard at his studies; but he found time to translate at least one long poem and to write a couple of plays. Moreover there are strong indications, of which you will find details in almost any biography of Marlowe, that when he came down from Cambridge, still at the age of twenty-three, he had been employed by the government on some kind of secret service work.

Everything about this incredibly gifted young man suggests a passionate, rebellious nature, enormous intellectual energy, and a kind of intoxicating inability to be moderate about anything: his atheism and his espionage, the louring splendour of his plays and the demonism of the leading characters, the filthy company he kept and his sordid and bloody death from a dagger-thrust in a Deptford pub at the age of twenty-nine, make it easy to cultivate romantic delusions about Marlowe. This is dangerous because we know very little about him apart from his plays.

Marlowe, then, left Cambridge and came to London in 1587. He had already placed *Tamburlaine* with the Earl of Leicester's players who were occupying The Curtain. This company was then managed by a certain Philip Henslowe who was to become the first theatrical manager in our history and the boss of the company that was to rival Shakespeare's. His leading actor was the great Edward Alleyn who is thought to have used a broad and rhetorical style of acting well suited to Marlowe's poetry. The other theatre, The Theatre, was run by the Burbage family, father, James, and sons, Cuthbert and Richard. Richard Burbage seems to have been a more versatile actor than Alleyn and with a style rather less in what we now call 'the grand manner'.

If it hadn't been for these two theatres it is almost inconceivable that Marlowe would have continued to be a dramatist. But Marlowe was lucky in the date of his birth and of his arrival in London for by 1587 the two theatres in Finsbury Fields had begun to attract the interest of the London intelligentsia. There must have been some exciting rivalry between the two young leading actors, Richard Burbage who was twenty, and Edward Alleyn a year older. More important still was the quality of the plays which were written for the two companies. 1587 saw the production of two plays by Robert Greene, one of which, *Alphonsus King of Aragon,* survives, George Peele's most impressive *David and Bethsabe,* and one of the great dramas of the Elizabethan age, Thomas Kyd's *The Spanish Tragedy*—together, of course, with *Tamburlaine* : a fine collection of plays.

What a group of young writers they were! Marlowe and Kyd were twenty-three, Greene was twenty-nine and Peele was thirty. They lived by and large on their wits and their pens. They wrote poems, pamphlets, plays, as the mood took them and opportunity arose. They lived with little regard for what we should call moral scruples. In an age that was seething with new ideas, they grasped the lot. They are described in many books as the 'University wits', but it is hard to think of a more inappropriate description for a group of young men who could hardly have done less honour to their Universities and who were passionate, romantic, satirical and sharptongued rather than witty.

The atmosphere of the England in which these young men passed their most impressionable years was poisoned by the intensity of the religious conflict. The skill and enthusiasm of leaders of the Reformed Church for torturing, maiming, burning and murdering Roman Catholics, was only equalled by the similar enthusiasm of Roman Catholics in dealing with Protestants when they were the top-dogs. But although the Protestants were masters in England they lived in intense fear of a Spanish invasion; and it was not many months after the production of

Tamburlaine that England was indeed saved from what might have been the bloodiest of all invasions by the skill of the men who defeated the Spanish Armada.

Into an England that was already seething with new ideas, more ideas came pouring from the Continent. So small a part do the works of the Greek and Roman authors play in the consciousness of people of our own age that it is difficult to realize the effect of the works of Homer, Aristotle, Virgil and Livy upon those who came upon them in the fifteenth and sixteenth centuries and read them with a kind of intoxicated excitement. Writers, scholars, churchmen, teachers found that these ancient books which were now being translated into vernacular languages for the first time threw open to them a whole new world of human experience, new literature, new myths, new stories, new theories, new points of view. English scholars did not on the whole become as fanatical in pursuit of these ideas as some of their French and Italian colleagues, but Marlowe, Jonson, and Shakespeare himself, even though he was despised by some of his contemporaries for knowing 'little Latin and less Greek', were all thoroughly imbued with this spirit.

It is thought by some critics that the book which had the greatest effect upon Marlowe was *The Prince,* the work of a not very successful Florentine diplomat by the name of Niccolò Machiavelli. Some people consider *The Prince* to be a text-book in all the political deceit and dishonesty which we associate with the name of Machiavelli; but for others it remains a serious scientific treatise on politics, liberating Renaissance princes from the stuffy theological notions of the Middle Ages. Scholars are undecided whether dramatists like Marlowe and Shakespeare were influenced by this book but its popularity does seem to explain why so many Elizabethan dramatists set the scene of their tragedies in the corrupt courts of the Italian princes. Although Marlowe did not do this he puts the Prologue to *The Jew of Malta* into the mouth of Machiavelli who says, roughly speaking, that he has come to England to teach the islanders a few of his ideas, unpopular though they are. But as the play has really very little to do with Machiavellianism I can't help feeling that Marlowe was merely being a little *risqué*, a little daring, teasing his audience with the prospect of a play which is shocking enough without an introduction by a Florentine politician.

So Marlowe clearly approached the theatre with a seething mind, and what a torrent of passion we find in his great political play *Tamburlaine*. Marlowe never beats about the bush. He has little use for political intrigue or the interplay of character. When the play was printed in 1590 its full title read :

Tamburlaine the Great, who from a Scythian shepherd, by his rare and wonderful Conquests, became a most puissant and mighty Monarche. And (for his Tyranny and Terror in War) was termed The Scourge of God.

The audience at the first performance of this play must have been pretty astounded when the Prologue entered and addressed them in the following tremendous words :

From jigging veins of rhyming mother wits,
And such conceits as clownage keeps in pay,
We'll lead you to the stately tent of war,

Where you shall hear the Scythian Tamburlaine
Threatening the world with high astounding terms,
And scourging kingdoms with his conquering sword.
View but his picture in this tragic glass,
And then applaud his fortune as you please.

And then follows what a surge of murder and massacre, what a tempest of high astounding terms and mighty lines! Who would not get carried away by stuff like this:

Meander: Your Majesty shall shortly have your wish,
             And ride in triumph through Persepolis.
Tamburlaine: And ride in triumph through Persepolis.
             Is it not brave to be a king, Techelles,
             Usumcasane and Therimidas?
             Is it not passing brave to be a king,
             And ride in triumph through Persepolis?
Techelles: O my lord, 'tis sweet and full of pomp.
Usumcasane: To be a king is half to be a god.
Therimidas: A god is not so glorious as a king . . .

Even the proper names help to carry one into a half-mythical Asiatic world of barbaric splendour over which the Scythian conqueror strides with a pitiless demonism, committing defeated kings to a cage which he uses as his footstool and at the height of his conquests entering in a chariot drawn by a couple of captive monarchs.

But Tamburlaine was the slave of passion, as we would say today, and the man who was only conquered by death itself, was submissive to Zenocrate. Here is one of the passages in which he invokes the beauty of this woman:

If all the pens that ever poets held
Had fed the feeling of their masters' thoughts,

And every sweetness that inspired their hearts,
Their minds, and muses on admired themes;
If all the heavenly quintessence they [di-] still
From their immortal flowers of poesy,
Wherein, as in a mirror, we perceive
The highest reaches of a human wit;
If these had made one poem's period,
And all combined in beauty's worthiness,
Yet should there hover in their restless heads
One thought, one grace, one wonder, at the least,
Which into words no virtue can digest.

Yet when Marlowe comes to write a second part he has further marvels. As Tamburlaine sits beside the dying Zenocrate he cries out against the iniquity of heaven to allow the death of the girl:

Black is the beauty of the brightest day,

he starts, and then his anger spent:

Now walk the angels on the walls of Heaven
As sentinels to warn the immortal souls
To entertain divine Zenocrate.

And how when the girl dies he blazes into vengeance:

So burn the turrets of this cursed town,
Flame to the highest region of the air,
And kindle heaps of exhalations,
That being fiery meteors may presage
Death and destruction to the inhabitants!

Marlowe's next play was *The Jew of Malta*, savage in its anti-semitism and even more savage in its view of the Christians. It is a lurid, pitiless, belly-rumbling affair, just to the taste of Elizabethan audiences who might watch an execution on their way to the theatre, pausing to appreciate the skill of the executioner in slicing his victim into quarters and removing the heart; and watching *Twelfth Night* perhaps against the screams of tormented animals from the Bear Pit scarcely fifty yards from the Globe. *The Jew of Malta* would undoubtedly be effective on the stage but whether, with our queasier tastes, we should enjoy its savagery is very doubtful.

Marlowe's fourth play, following in quick succession, was *The Massacre at Paris: with the Death of the Duke of Guise.* This play is never reckoned among Marlowe's masterpieces. He wrote it almost certainly in haste : action follows action without premeditation, without even those tremendous billows of poetry that lift the audience or the reader into the world of Marlowe's imagination; and the characters which ride so often on the splendour of the verse are neither splendid nor convincing. Yet the play is interesting because it enables us to see the wheels go round, to see something of what Marlowe's imaginative world was like when the poet wasn't lit by his own genius. Thus speaks the Duke of Guise in his first soliloquy :

> *What glory is there in a common good*
> *That hangs for every peasant to achieve?*
> *That like I best that flies beyond my reach.*
> *Set me to scale the high Pyramides*
> *And thereon set the diadem of France.*

And so with an unscrupulous brutishness Guise plunges into a monstrous succession of murders, deceits, acts of hatred and revenge, that are both sickening and laughable.

Marlowe's next play was *The Troublesome reign and lamentable death of Edward the Second, King of England: with the Tragical Fall of proud Mortimer*. This play is different from anything else of Marlowe's and in some ways it is hard to relate it to the author of *Tamburlaine, The Jew of Malta* and *Dr. Faustus*. It is the only play of Marlowe's in which his preoccupation with characters who are driven on by demonism to excesses of behaviour has loosened its grip on him. The play is about the young king Edward II and his deep but extremely unpopular love for his favourite courtier Piers Gaveston. It is also about Edward's relationship with his wife and the group of young noblemen, headed by Mortimer, who partly because they are themselves ambitious but also because they are genuinely concerned at the effect of Edward's behaviour on the country, rebel against him, capture and imprison him, and have him murdered. The final scenes in Kenilworth Castle are among the most moving that Marlowe ever wrote and are continually compared with the last act of Shakespeare's *Richard II*. Some people believe that Shakespeare was influenced by Marlowe, as Marlowe, they think, was influenced by Shakespeare's early plays, especially the three parts of *Henry VI*.

Here I would like to warn my readers of our serious lack of information about the Elizabethan drama, so much so that anyone trying to arrive at a definite date for the first performance or publication of an Elizabethan play will be bewildered by the conflicting theories. The three parts of *Henry VI* are an example of this. There is extreme uncertainty as to when they were written and even, surprisingly, by whom.

The whole question of the authorship of many Elizabethan plays is a complicated one. We know from the detailed *Diary* which Philip Henslowe kept for many years that some Elizabethan plays were written by as many as four authors, each writing an act, or a few scenes at a guinea an act. We know that at one time Ben Jonson was commissioned by Henslowe to write some additional scenes for *The Spanish Tragedy*; and all the dramatists, Shakespeare included, were quite unscrupulous about basing their plays, when occasion arose, on older and simpler versions of a story that attracted them. That is why experts often find traces of the style of several different dramatists in a single play, and why the authorship, even of the works of Shakespeare, is disputed. So we find that Marlowe from time to time is credited with having written the whole or parts of quite a number of other Elizabethan plays and of at least two of which even the titles are lost. An American professor has gone so far as to claim that Marlowe not only wrote his own plays but the complete works of Shakespeare into the bargain. It is frequently said that such literary detective work is unimportant so long as we have the plays. I find this a curiously unappetizing point of view. If one really enjoys the plays it is surely a matter of the greatest possible interest to know who wrote them.

Marlowe's last play, *Dr Faustus*, is plagued with similar doubts about its authorship. The opening and closing scenes are authentic Marlowe. But one cannot help questioning the middle scenes of the play and how they came to be written by a man of Marlowe's ability. Marlowe has drawn another of his demonic characters, a man possessed by a lust for knowledge and a knowledge that will give him power. Dr Faustus was a well-known German character of the Middle Ages of whose compact with the Devil many stories were told in a book published during Marlowe's lifetime. At the beginning of the play Marlowe shows Faustus searching in the ancient books of the Greeks and the Romans for the secret of power :

Couldst thou make men to live eternally,
Or, being dead, raise them to life again,
Then this profession [that of scholar] *were to be esteemed.*

And a little later in the same speech :

O what a world of profit and delight,
Of power, of honour, of omnipotence
Is promised to the studious artisan!
All things that move between the quiet poles
Shall be at my command: emperors and kings
Are but obeyed in their several provinces,
Nor can they raise the wind or rend the clouds;
But his dominion that exceeds in this
Stretcheth as far as doth the mind of man,
A sound magician is a mighty god.

Faustus tries 'the uttermost magic can perform' and Mephistophilis enters. The scene which then takes place in the clarity and power of its thought, the strength of its verse, and in sheer theatrical excitement, is one of the finest that Marlowe ever wrote. And then the play nose-dives into a sort of pantomimic world of practical jokes which are only relieved by the splendid vision of Helen and the great speech beginning :

Was this the face that launched a thousand ships
And burnt the topless towers of Ilium?

5

Line after line and scene after scene appear to be debunking black magic and the existence of Mephistophilis : but when the twenty-four years of the compact are up and Faustus is back in his study Marlowe pulls out every stop to create the despair and frenzy of a man who is consigned to Hell; and in case there should be anyone in the audience not willing to take the thing seriously, the Chorus ends the play with the words :

> . . . *regard his hellish fall,*
> *Whose fiendful fortune may exhort the wise*
> *Only to wonder at unlawful things,*
> *Whose deepness doth entice such forward wits*
> *To practise more than heavenly power permits.*

On May 30th, 1593, in the most puzzling circumstances, Marlowe was stabbed to death in a pub in Deptford. He was twenty-nine. Know-alls and moralists, of whom there are always plenty kicking around, have been quick to apply the words I have just quoted to Marlowe himself. Without doubt he is the most bewildering, provocative, tantalizing character in the history of British drama, and with the possible exception of Shakespeare perhaps the most gifted. If he squandered his gifts practising more than heavenly power permits, his end was as brutal and abrupt as that of any of the characters he created.

SOME BOOKS FOR FURTHER READING :

It is understandable that a lot of people should have had a crack at unravelling this mysterious character though I would recommend my readers to avoid books with titles that suggest their authors would have done better to write a work of fiction. I have in mind *The Muse's Darling* and *And Morning in His Eyes*. The author of the latter book, Philip Henderson, went on to repent and write an excellent short biography simply called *Christopher Marlowe*. Good books with the same title have been written by F. S. Boas, John Bakeless, Una Ellis-Fermor, J. M. Robertson, and Michel Poirier. Harry Levin's *The Overreacher* is rather theoretical and has little biography. There are probably many more, but when you have read these together with Marlowe's Collected Works you'll know a good deal about the man.

The theory that Marlowe wrote the plays of Shakespeare is developed by Calvin Hoffman in a book called *The Murder of the Man Who Was Shakespeare*.

Marlowe's best plays are well printed in the Mermaid edition. The Everyman edition, though in small print, is complete. A 'potted' version of the two parts of *Tamburlaine* as it was produced at the Old Vic in 1951 is published by Heinemann. Most of the plays are obtainable separately in various editions.

CHAPTER FIVE

William Shakespeare

I AM GOING TO begin this chapter by putting down the known facts about the life of William Shakespeare.

He was born on April 23rd, 1564, at Stratford-on-Avon. He was thus the same age as Marlowe.

On November 27th, 1582, a William Shakespere (note the spelling) married an Anne Whateley in the Parish Church in Worcester; but the next day, November 28th, there is application by a William Shagspere to marry an Anne Hathaway in the same church. (The most ingenious theories are continually being advanced to explain this extraordinary situation.)

Six months later a daughter was born to Anne Hathaway, not Miss Whateley; and eighteen months later a twin boy and girl.

In 1594 Shakespeare is named among a company of actors who presented a couple of comedies in front of Queen Elizabeth.

In 1596 he was living on Bankside, south of the Thames, and near the Globe Theatre where some of his greatest plays were first staged. It was in this same year that he applied to the College of Heralds, on his father's behalf, for a coat-of-arms; and for £60 he bought the famous Stratford property of New Place. He was clearly doing well in the world.

In 1599 the Globe Theatre was opened on Bankside. Shakespeare became a shareholder in the theatre together with the Burbage brothers and four other actors.

In 1602 he bought more land in Stratford. In 1603 he is known to have acted in Ben Jonson's *Sejanus*.

We have a number of other references to small legal and financial transactions from this period, but they add nothing to our knowledge of him as a man, a dramatist, or a poet.

He died on April 25th, 1616, leaving a will in which he makes a large number of detailed behests, dismisses his wife with the 'second-best bed and the furniture' and leaves the rest to his son-in-law. Of references to books, manuscripts or anything whatsoever connected with the full literary life he must have led, there are none.

To sum up: all we really know about Shakespeare is that he was born of a well-to-do Warwickshire family, married in haste and under necessity, came up to London and became a successful though not an outstanding actor, and around the year 1610 retired to his native Stratford-on-Avon where he lived till he died.

Although he must have been one of the most notable figures in London between the years 1595 and 1610 there does not exist one single contemporary reference to William Shakespeare as a dramatist; and although the Shakespeares were a distinguished Stratford family there is not a single tradition in the town that refers to the literary activities of her greatest citizen.

In 1623, seven years after his death, a collected edition of his plays was published under the editorship of his two fellow actors, John Heminge and Henry Condell. This volume is known as the *First Folio*. It contains thirty-six plays. Some of these plays are now thought not to have been the work of Shakespeare—*Henry VIII*, for instance; but the volume does not include *Pericles* which is now generally considered to be authentic. Of these thirty-six plays only sixteen had appeared in print before 1623. Of these sixteen plays only nine bear Shakespeare's name on the title page. Some of Shakespeare's greatest plays were printed for the first time in the *First Folio*. These include *Twelfth Night, Julius Caesar, Macbeth,* and *Antony and Cleopatra*. But nine plays appeared during his lifetime with his name on the title-page which do not appear in the *First Folio*.

Modern scholars have tended to criticize Heminge and Condell for the careless manner in which they carried out their editorial responsibilities: they do not appear always to have chosen the best available version of the play although they claim to have done so, and there are many inaccuracies in the way the plays have been printed; but we must remember that if it hadn't been for their enterprise the four plays I have just mentioned, which are among the masterpieces of dramatic literature, would almost certainly have been lost to us for ever.

I have given these rather depressing facts at some length because it is important to realize what an enormous amount that is written about Shakespeare is conjecture. When we are not even sure which plays are indisputably his own work, which he had a hand in, and which he is credited with having written but didn't, there is enormous scope for literary detective work. This partially explains the enormous number of books on Shakespeare that appear yearly.

If Marlowe's violent plays and atheistical convictions

suggest a smouldering irascible young man, Shakespeare's are surely the work of a witty, passionate, aristocratic fellow. I have suggested that Marlowe responded to the seething anxieties of his times by creating protagonists who were possessed by a sense of human power and plunged headlong to the very frontiers of human experience. But Shakespeare not only gave voice to the passions of a passionate age but has set forth in his plays, more fully than almost any other writer has ever done, a kind of commentary upon this strange complicated animal which is Man. He painted on broader canvases than Marlowe did and he treated a greater range of subjects. He also mixed his colours less garishly. Shakespeare's plays are written with so rich and varied an understanding of human nature that men and women continue to delve into them for a lifetime and still find new treasures, new meanings, and new interpretations. This is the second reason for the enormous number of books that are written about Shakespeare and his plays.

And in just the same way many and many a book about Shakespeare starts off by saying something very similar to what I have said here. But the fact remains that you can't say anything about Shakespeare without establishing at the start that the man is a very prodigy.

Put very simply Shakespeare is far and away the world's most popular dramatist. Year after year in goodness knows how many languages the production of Shakespeare's plays represents the highest achievement of the leading companies. Producers, actors and actresses find in his plays the profoundest challenge to their genius and audiences their richest theatrical experience.

The fact is that for all the attention that has been

paid him by critics, philosophers and scholars, Shakespeare was firstly a dramatist; and although there are people who prefer to read his plays at home than to see them on the stage—and nothing is more exasperating than to hear your favourite passage mangled by a weak actor, we must accept the authentic fact that Shakespeare was a busy professional dramatist who wrote his plays to earn a livelihood for himself and the members of the Lord Chamberlain's Company. Shakespeare's plays are not easy to act; but I think that most people who are able to visit a theatre will agree that a successful performance of a Shakespeare play is an unforgettable experience.

If then we agree that Shakespeare was a dramatist before he was a poet, let me confine what I have to say to the methods he used in writing plays. There are three aspects of his genius that I would like to comment on and the first is what I might call the meaning of his plays.

I do not mean by this that I am going to slog through the thirty-six plays and describe what seems to me to be their meaning when many people have written a book about a single play and still not covered all the possibilities.

My purpose is quite simply and practically to point out to you that Shakespeare's plays, in common with the plays of many other dramatists, have a theme, a subject, or an idea, that is not directly explained by the story; that this theme or subject is something that every intelligent play-goer should reason out for himself; that whenever he sees the play he should try to decide what the producer and the actors have considered this theme to be, and whether they have succeeded in realizing it consistently. This exciting mental exercise is the only way of appreciating what one might call the 'interpretation' of the plays. I will give a couple of examples of what I mean.

When Sir Laurence Olivier made a film of *Hamlet* he flashed upon the screen at the beginning: 'This is the tragedy of a man who could not make up his mind', or words to that effect. *Hamlet*, as you know, is the story of a young Prince who meets his father's ghost upon the castle battlements at night and learns how he, his father, has been murdered by his brother, Hamlet's uncle, who is now king. Hamlet is told by the Ghost that he must revenge his father's murder. Sir Laurence is evidently impressed by the fact that it takes Hamlet another four acts to work himself up to do it.

This does not seem to me to be the point of the play at all. Reading carefully the first few scenes one finds that procrastination is not the most important element that emerges. Long before the Ghost has told Hamlet of his uncle's guilt Shakespeare has begun to emphasize that 'everything is rotten in the state of Denmark', that Hamlet is a sensitive young Prince in the middle of a corrupt court and that he is seething with indignation at the behaviour of his mother who has married her brother-in-law within two months of her husband's death. Hamlet's disgust at his mother's precipitate and tasteless action is the subject of his first and one of his most violent soliloquies, beginning:

> *O that this too, too solid flesh would melt,*
> *Thaw, and resolve itself into a dew . . .*

If therefore you agree with Sir Laurence Olivier that the most important theme in *Hamlet* is the procrastination of the Prince, you will expect the actor's interpretation to be quite different from what it would be if he were following my own suggestion which is that *Hamlet* is about the moral responsibilities of a young man who finds himself involved in an atmosphere of evil and corruption.

I do not suggest for a moment that this is the correct or even the only interpretation of *Hamlet*. There are many valid interpretations and every actor makes his own. But I want to suggest that to understand a Shakespeare play properly it's not enough simply to be able to write the story of the play on a post card : these plays are packed with meaning that only becomes clear when you prod about for it.

Let me give another example. I remember having read in the books that I used to be made to read that *Othello* is about jealousy and *Macbeth* about ambition. These interpretations may be true but they don't take us very far towards understanding the plays and they are certainly of little help to the actors. Let's consider *Macbeth* for a moment. A victorious general is returning from battle with the Norwegians when upon a 'blasted heath' he is met by the prophetic greetings of three witches. When he next writes to his wife he gives her a simple description of what has happened. The witches had greeted him as 'Thane of Cawdor', 'Thane of Glamis', and 'King that shalt be'. Hardly has Lady Macbeth finished reading the letter and a messenger has announced that Duncan, king of Scotland, is coming to spend the night in her castle, than she has become the murderess. Of course, because she's ambitious. But plenty of people are ambitious without being murderers, and her words are more than those of an ambitious woman :

> . . . *The raven himself is hoarse*
> *That croaks the fatal entrance of Duncan*
> *Under my battlements. Come, you spirits*
> *That tend on mortal thoughts, unsex me here,*
> *And fill me, from the crown to the toe, top-full*
> *Of direst cruelty.*

They are not the words of an ambitious woman but of an evil woman and it seems to me far more profitable to consider *Macbeth* as a study in evil than in ambition.

Let me repeat then that one of the first ways of getting on terms with Shakespeare is to read his serious plays and to try to decide what they are about. Besides *Hamlet* and *Macbeth* there is considerable 'meaning in depth' to be discovered in *Othello, King Lear* (what a play!), *Timon of Athens, Measure for Measure* (a difficult but fascinating play), *The Merchant of Venice* (of which I shall have more to say), *Troilus and Cressida* (another perplexing and provocative play), and *Julius Caesar*. In some ways the comedies are a little more difficult.

I do not want to suggest that the only meaning I think a play can have is a kind of rational meaning that can be worked out as I have worked out the meaning of *Hamlet* and *Macbeth*. Although it would be possible to argue that *Twelfth Night* is a play about different kinds of love, the passionate but unreciprocated love of the Duke Orsino for the lovely young Olivia, the sudden impulsive love of Olivia for Viola who is dressed as a boy, the love that at all costs must be concealed of Viola for the Duke, and finally the self-love of Malvolio, I fancy that Shakespeare based his comedies not upon some deep preoccupation, but upon a comic situation or a group of characters. Surely what fascinated Shakespeare increasingly in *A*

Midsummer Night's Dream was the fun and the enchantment to be discovered in weaving a play out of three
groups of characters all of whom for one reason or another
are passing the night in an enchanted wood, the fairies
who live there and have their own rivalries and quarrels,
the mortal lovers who flee to the wood to escape their
parents, and the group of workmen, led by Bottom, who
go to a clearing in the wood to rehearse the play they
are to act before the Duke. Once Shakespeare had got as
far as that, and invented the wonderful character of Puck
who weaves the thread of misunderstanding round the
three groups of characters, what fun he must have had in
working it out.

With that I leave it to the honour of you, my readers,
to turn at once to *Love's Labour Lost,* to *As You Like It,*
and to the magnificent histories in which some of Shakespeare's richest characterizations are to be found, and to
read them as if you were under an obligation to distil
from them the very essence of their meaning and their
artistic quality.

I now come to my second subject, that is Shakespeare's
use of language. Of course the words are important. Most
plays only exist in the words in which they are written and
no two dramatists write dialogue exactly alike. But Shakespeare is the supreme poetic dramatist of the English
language and I will try to explain what this means. Let me
take an example again from *Hamlet.*

In the second scene, which is set in the throne-room of
the palace of Elsinore, Claudius, the king, informs his
court of his marriage to Queen Gertrude and then goes on
to tell them that their country is threatened by the Nor-
wegian Prince Fortinbras. Having dealt with the business

of the day the King looks at Hamlet and asks him why he continues to be so depressed. Hamlet turns the question aside with a quick sharp answer. His Mother takes him up. Why does he still mourn his father, she asks,

> *Thou know'st 'tis common, all that lives must die,*
> *Passing through nature to eternity.*
> Hamlet: *Ay, Madam, it is common.*
> Queen: *If it be,*
> *Why seems it so particular with thee?*
> Hamlet: *Seems, Madam? nay, it is: I know not seems:*
> *'Tis not alone my inky cloak, good Mother,*
> *Nor customary suits of solemn black,*
> *Nor windy suspiration of forc'd breath* [sighs]
> *No, nor the fruitful river in the eye* [tears]
> *Nor the dejected haviour of the visage,*
> *Together with all forms, moods, shows of grief,*
> *That can denote me truly. These indeed seem,*
> *For they are actions that a man might play:*
> *But I have that within which passeth show;*
> *These, but the trappings and the suits of woe.*

Say these lines aloud. You will find that in spite of the difficult metaphors they run very easily off the tongue. They are perfectly courteous as befits a young man speaking to the King his uncle, but they are deliberately a little obscure. Hamlet has clearly no intention of telling his uncle or his Mother what he thinks of them. So we find the sense is perfectly allied to the form of the verse, the quick, smooth, courteous rhythm, the touch of formality in the long balanced phrases, and the slower beat of the last two very moving lines, which he really says to himself.

A moment later the court moves out and Hamlet is left alone. Suddenly he bursts out in the famous words:

O that this too too solid flesh would melt,
Thaw, and resolve itself into a dew:
Or that the Everlasting had not fix'd
His Canon 'gainst self-slaughter. O God, O God!
How weary, stale, flat, and unprofitable
Seems to me all the uses of this world!
Fie on't! oh fie, fie, 'tis an unweeded garden
That grows to seed: things rank and gross in nature
Possess it merely. That it should come to this:
But two months dead: nay, not so much; not two,
So excellent a King that was to this
Hyperion to a satyr . . .

Do you see the difference? This is all short explosive phrases. Every line is broken in the middle, sometimes more than once. The words are short and hard, very different from the long rolling and slightly difficult phrases with which Hamlet addresses his mother. And so it goes on until the end of the speech. Is not this a wonderful example of the language of desperation? Of fury? Of almost intolerable grief? Do you see how an actor only need respond to the rhythms that Shakespeare has given him to have much of the situation created for him. It is this perfect harmony between the dramatic significance of the scene and the language he gives his characters that makes Shakespeare a supreme dramatic poet, and what is even more unique, for Browning was that, a supreme poetic dramatist.

Let me give another example, this time from *Macbeth*. When we first meet Lady Macbeth she is reading the letter from her husband in which he recounts his meeting with the Witches and how they greeted him 'Thane of Cawdor' and 'King that shalt be'. Hardly has she finished the letter than her mind runs to murder.

Glamis thou art, and Cawdor, and shalt be
What thou art promised: yet do I fear thy nature;
It is too full of the milk of human kindness
To catch the nearest way [by murder]; *thou wouldst be*
  great,
Art not without ambition, but without
The illness should attend it [by illness she means roughly
  unscrupulousness]; *what thou wouldst highly,*
That wouldst thou holily [suggesting Macbeth is a
  religious man]; *wouldst not play false*
And yet wouldst wrongly win [the despicable sort who
  won't cheat himself but won't protest at anyone else
  cheating even to the benefiting from it].
                    Thou 'ldst have, great Glamis,
That which cries, ' Thus thou must do, if thou have it;
And that which rather thou dost fear to do
Than wishest should be undone.'

Doesn't this shrewd and close-packed analysis of her
husband's character tell us a lot about him and even more
about her? Can you see how superby actable they are, these
quiet quick broken lines of a woman whose mind is racing
towards the accomplishment of a ghastly murder? For me
the supremacy of Shakespeare is won by innumerable
passages such as this rather than by the intrinsic quality of
his poetry, magnificent though it is.

The third subject I would like to touch on concerns the
visual side of Shakespeare's plays. The most notable event
in the early years of the Lord Chamberlain's Company
occurred in 1599 when having quarrelled with the landlord
of The Theatre the actors tore down the building, trans-
ported the timber across the river and constructed the
Globe on the South Bank. The morality of such an action
remains questionable, but its importance for the future of

the English theatre is not in doubt. We don't know any details of the Globe Theatre at first hand but we have the exact specifications of the Fortune which Philip Henslowe built very near the Globe. We know that the two theatres were similar because Philip Henslowe ensured this by quite simply employing the same carpenter, one Peter Street. Thus we know that the Globe was octagonal in shape, that it had a large stage thrust into the middle of the pit, and that the audience stood on three sides of it. These were the famous 'groundlings' who had paid the cheapest price of admission. Around the walls of the theatre were three galleries. At the back of the stage there was a recess and above it a gallery which was used both by musicians and the players. On each side of the stage were doors, one of which led to the actors Tiring or Dressing Room.

This large platform stage, as it is now called, was not suitable for the use of scenery. The architecture of the stage and of the recess and gallery behind it was in the same style as that of the auditorium. References by foreigners to the splendour of English theatres suggest that they must have been particularly brightly painted. The important point is that there was no strong distinction between the architecture of the stage and of the auditorium. The whole theatre was a single architectural unit within which a play was acted upon a raised platform. Since the whole theatre was open to the sky there was not even an artificial distinction between stage and auditorium created by means of lights.

The advantages and the snags of acting on a platform stage have been hotly discussed in recent years. A good deal of attention has been given to experiments in presenting the plays of Shakespeare in conditions as near as

VIII   Elizabethan London

IX   A reconstruction of Elizabethan London

X   The Globe Theatre

possible to those of the Globe. That Shakespeare's plays are particularly well suited to performance on an 'apron-stage' most people I think will agree, and as it's the sort of theatre for which he wrote it isn't very surprising.

Why then are Shakespeare's plays best suited for performance on a stage very different from our own?

Because they have a rare mixture of intimacy and spaciousness. To deliver a soliloquy convincingly an actor needs close contact with at least one part of his audience. To deliver the more rhetorical parts he needs a large audience and good-sized acting-area or stage. Both these conditions the Globe, with the vast audience on three sides of the stage and the open sky above, provided.

Then Shakespeare recognizes no discipline with regard to time and place. Scene follows scene taking the imagination of the audience from Alexandra to Rome and back again in a moment, jumping twenty-five years in a line of verse. Scene must follow scene without the smallest break if the essential continuity is not to be lost. This was only possible in a theatre that dispensed with scenery.

Contrary to what has sometimes been suggested Shakespeare very rarely mentions the scenery or setting of his plays. In *Macbeth* the King, Duncan, comments upon the charm of the castle before he enters it, not to tell the audience that it is a pleasant place but to add irony to its being the scene of his murder. Shakespeare does something far more satisfactory than work descriptions of the scenery into his text which might have the effect of slowing the pace of the action. He weaves into his plays a large number of vivid adjectives, phrases, and metaphors which create the imaginative world in which his play is taking place. I will give two examples of what I mean.

6

Twelfth Night, as I have already said, is a play about love. It takes place in an enchanted and enchanting country of the imagination called Illyria, which Shakespeare never describes by so much as a single word. Perhaps the most exquisite scene in the play is that in which Viola, disguised as a page, visits the Countess Olivia to tell her how much her master, the Duke Orsino, is in love with her. Olivia will have none of these protestations from a man she cannot and will not love. Viola says she finds it hard to believe that so lovely a girl as Olivia can be so disinterested in the advances of so admirable a man as Orsino. If I were in your place, she says, I would not act as you are doing. What would you do? asks Olivia. And Viola answers:

> (I'd) *Make me a willow-cabin at your gate,*
> *And call upon my soul within the house,*
> *Write loyal cantons of contemned love*
> *And sing them loud even at the dead of night;*
> *Hallo your name to the reverberate hills*
> *And make the babbling gossips of the air*
> *Cry out, Olivia.*

The dramatic purpose of this speech, or of this aria as I would like to call it, is to express the ecstasy of a young girl who is wildly in love. But by the use of such epithets as 'willow cabin', 'loyal cantons', 'contemned love', 'reverberate hills', 'dead of night', 'babbling gossips of the air', and similar images scattered throughout the play, Shakespeare not only creates, in this case, the intensely poetic nature of Viola's character, but an atmosphere of distant hills and meadows filled with flowers, of willows growing by the banks of streams and of the song of birds in the early morning light, in short, a land where the characters who appear in *Twelfth Night* might be expected to live and where the events in which they become involved might be expected to take place.

Let me take my second example from *The Merchant of Venice*. As a matter of fact there is an example in this play of a case where Shakespeare does describe the scene; and while it is memorable poetry, dramatically it is a failure. Jessica and Lorenzo, a pair of young lovers, are wandering through the moonlit garden of Portia's house in Belmont.

How sweet the moonlight sleeps upon this bank Lorenzo says and proceeds to settle down with his beloved on the edge of a hard and uncomfortable-looking rostrum. But when he forgets the bank and starts to talk about the stars—

> *. . . Look how the floor of heaven*
> *Is thick inlaid with patens of bright gold*

it's fine, because we have to imagine the stars, unless the designer, as so often happens, has taken it into his head to reproduce the milky-way on the back-cloth.

Here is another example from *The Merchant of Venice*. The play, you may remember, concerns a group of merchants, one of whom, a certain Antonio, borrows three thousand ducats from the Jew Shylock against the return of some of his merchant ships. The drama of the play turns upon the reported loss of Antonio's fleet and hence his inability to repay Shylock. After a short opening speech in which Antonio speaks of how unaccountably melancholy he is, two of his friends try to cheer him up with these golden words :

Your mind is tossing on the Ocean
There where your argosies with portly sail
Like signiors and rich burghers on the flood
Or as it were the pageants of the sea,
Do overpeer the petty traffickers
That curt'sy to them, do them reverence
As they fly by them with their woven wings.

No, not golden words, but salty words, billowing, belly-ing words, salt-spray-and-spume-of-the-sea words that douche the imagination of the spectator with images of stately merchant ships, their holds loaded with merchandise for Venice . . . words which since they set the scene must be superbly spoken (all too often they are not because the characters who speak them are not considered effective parts and so are usually played by less distinguished mem-bers of the company!)

This aspect of Shakespeare's technique does set appal-ling problems for scene-designers who have to create a setting for the play which will harmonize with the inter-pretation of the play, be visually satisfying, and yet will not distract the attention of the audience from words which if they are well spoken and well listened to will touch the imagination of the audience more deeply than the most skilful attempt to call up the Rialto in Venice from half a dozen buckets of distemper on a well-primed canvas.

From all this one fact is inescapable. The performance of a Shakespeare play cannot be wholly successful unless the text is extremely well spoken; and as I have already said, extremely well listened to. In various works Pro-fessor Bertram Joseph of Bristol University has advanced certain theories about Elizabethan actors and their audi-ences, suggesting that through their training in rhetoric, their close familiarity with the language of Shakespeare, and the acute attention of their audiences, Burbage and his fellows were able to achieve effects with words far beyond anything we can do today. Two facts alone induce me to believe that we are infants in the speaking of Shakespeare : one is that for Elizabethan audiences Shakespeare was not a highbrow but the most popularly successful dramatist of his day; and the second is the extraordinary fact that throughout the Elizabethan theatres and without exception, all the women's parts were played by boys—so far as we can tell, with complete success.

I shall end on a note of heresy. Scholars in the Universities are giving increasing attention to the plays of Shakespeare, not less. The number of books on the dramatist shows no sign of lessening. Every aspect of his genius has been analysed, tabulated, recorded, discussed. Pages are written and battles are fought over a single word. But Shakespeare, as I must emphasize, was a worker in the theatre. He was a practising dramatist. It's silly to pretend that his plays are not full of inaccuracies and inconsistencies. I could quote a hundred, starting off with the shocking and rather disgusting legal casuistry by which Portia turns the tables on the vindictive Shylock. Sometimes Shakespeare is perfunctory in tying up his plots. The last act of *The Merchant of Venice* is a masterpiece, but that of *Twelfth Night* is a thoroughly careless job. Shakespeare is continually clumsy and sometimes boring. At times he was doubtless rushed. The play was wanted urgently, Burbage must have an additional speech, the theatre is merciless to its servants. Yet I have seen poets working in the theatre and the best of them will scribble an extra verse on the back of a packet of cigarettes. That's being master of your Muse—as you should be. Shakespeare hardly wrote a stage-direction in his life. He rarely even divided his plays into scenes and acts and when he did he did it inconsistently.

Yet there was a tradition in the seventeenth century that Shakespeare 'never blotted out a line in his life', and Ben Jonson, in a rather unconvincing introduction to the *First Folio* says : 'His mind and hand went together. And what he thought, he uttered with that easiness, that we have scarce received from him a blot in his papers.' This suggests that Shakespeare often wrote, as we should suppose, at white heat, that he had a natural facility that never deserted him, and, as seems to me most likely, that the conditions of the theatre often robbed him of opportunity for revision. But to suggest that he never wrote a dull speech, that he never committed an error in the construction of his plots, that he is always and absolutely peerless, is not to honour his memory but to become idolatrous, and to rob him of that quality that shines and blazes through his plays and for which he is often loved before all else, his humanity.

SOME BOOKS FOR FURTHER READING :

There are innumerable books about Shakespeare, but I have found these particularly interesting. Ivor Brown—*Shakespeare*. Henri Fluchère—*Shakespeare*. J. Middleton Murray —*Shakespeare*. John Masefield—*William Shakespeare*. J. Dover Wilson—*The Essential Shakespeare*.

There are two admirable collections of essays on many different aspects of Shakespeare—Harley Granville Barker and G. B. Harrison's *Companion to Shakespeare Studies* and John Garrett's *Talking of Shakespeare*. Allardyce Nicoll's annual *Shakespeare Survey* is always full of good things. Best of all perhaps is Margaret Webster's *Shakespeare Today*.

Good background material will be found in: J. Harbage's *Shakespeare's Audiences*, G. B. Harrison's *Elizabethan Plays and Players* (a great favourite of mine) and J. Dover Wilson's *Life in Shakespeare's England*.

And on the Elizabethan theatre I recommend: J. Walter Hodges's *The Globe Restored* (pictorial reconstruction) and Ronald Watkyn's *Moonlight at the Globe* and *On Producing Shakespeare*, admirable discussions on how plays were staged at the Globe.

There are some fine critical works on the plays: A. C. Bradley's *Shakespearian Tragedy*, Harley Granville Barker's *Prefaces to Shakespeare*, G. Wilson Knight's *The Wheel of Fire* and *The Imperial Theme*, A. Quiller-Couch's *Shakespeare's Workmanship*, and William Poel's *Shakespeare in the Theatre*.

The reading of Shakespeare's plays should be the greatest possible pleasure. There are far too many 'school' editions, some badly printed, others with a monstrous array of notes that reduce the text to a few pathetic lines pushed up to the top of each page. Eschew such editions or protest if you are asked to read them. Nor do I feel much enthusiasm for the omnibus editions (horrible expression!) which are far too heavy to be handled comfortably and printed tiresomely in double columns.

I do not mean by this little diatribe that notes are not important: they are invaluable; but in moderation. For clarity, economy, and pleasant handling it would be difficult to improve upon the Penguin edition.

CHAPTER SIX

Ben Jonson

BEN JONSON IS all flesh and blood. The facts of his life are not disputed, there is no question of the authorship of his plays, their intention is clear. Ben Jonson is a substantial character and as English as his name.

He was born in Westminster in 1572. His father, who was a poor minister, died a month before he was born. His mother married again, this time a poor bricklayer. This was unfortunate, for the many enemies which he made in the course of his life could never resist the joke.

A clever child living in Westminster was quite properly educated at Westminster School. Here he distinguished himself as a classical scholar.

Let me try to describe the curious character of Ben Jonson. He was a strong hefty fellow with heavy features. He had a turbulent, argumentative nature, picked quarrels readily, and resorted quickly to fighting. He had a brain that worked overtime, a rich store of classical learning—in his day he was thought to be the most learned man in England—and a prolific imagination. But whatever his enemies might say, however great his respect for classical perfection, he kept an instinctive sympathy for the low-life of London, the rogues and ragamuffins of the streets of Westminster, then little more than a country village, and the rich characters of a London fair-ground.

What is remarkable about Ben Jonson is that he succeeded in reconciling all these various and conflicting
elements in his character. His great plays are the product
of a tremendous brain. In fact I cannot think of a
single writer with the possible exception of Bernard Shaw
whose works make one so conscious of the power of the
intellect behind them. At the same time there is a
tremendous physical energy in his characters. They're all
living to the very top of their bent. They have big,
expressive, and often ugly voices. One pictures them as
so many caricatures with strong features, blotched com-
plexions, gangling limbs, obese or emaciated, the sort of
characters that make you terribly aware of their physical
existence, even of their smell. When he is writing a play
set in Imperial Rome, such as *Sejanus,* he forces his
characters into a sort of Roman dignity, but their brutish
strength remains.

Ben Jonson did not emerge as an integrated character
from the start. He had barely finished at Westminster
when, as a boy still in his teens, he was off to Flanders to
fight for William of Orange against the Spaniards. (We
suppose he wanted to escape working in a builder's yard.)
Flanders was the fashionable resort for ne'er-do-wells, for
aggressive personalities unable to find more constructive
outlets for their energy, and for those who held dearly
the cause of Protestant freedom against Spanish political
tyranny. Ben Jonson was not a ne'er-do-well, and he gives
no indications in his writings that he felt deeply about
religious or political persecution. He simply hadn't yet
found himself.

On his return to England he got work as an actor and a
writer—we can hardly call him dramatist—with Philip

Henslowe. He tinkered with other people's plays—it was at this period that he did some restorative work upon *The Spanish Tragedy*—and had a shot at writing his own. Meanwhile his irascibility breaks out all over the place. He had a hand in what was apparently a politically scurrilous play (unhappily now lost) called *The Isle of Dogs* for which he was imprisoned. (English theatre-managers now support the Censorship of plays simply because it is a guarantee against this sort of disaster.) When he was released he fell out with one of the members of the company, one Gabriel Spencer, and slew him in a duel. He was again imprisoned and only secured his release by evoking a curious Elizabethan law that pardoned educated men from hanging.

Having killed one of Henslowe's company he offered his next play to the Lord Chamberlain's men, the Shakespeare-Burbage company. There is a charming legend that Shakespeare had a hand in its acceptance. *Every Man In His Humour* was a great success. But Jonson's creative personality was still at sixes-and-sevens. Although a play about London and Londoners, he set it in Italy. The contradictions must have been obvious; for when in 1616 he issued a collected edition of his plays, and the London mood in which he had just written *Bartholomew Fair* was upon him, he re-wrote this play, setting it in the city.

Jonson was at odds with the world, not an uncommon stage of adolescence. They were not easy years for anybody. The great Queen was nearing her end and the possibility of a peaceful succession to the throne seemed to be remote. He slashed around at everything that displeased him from the behaviour of courtiers to the language used by tragic dramatists. The success of *Every*

Man In His Humour went to his head. He followed it with *Every Man Out of His Humour.* This is not so much a play as a kind of dramatic charade in which he caricatures some of the dramatists and personalities of the day in a highly stylish manner.

But Jonson was not the only high-spirited and outspoken young dramatist of the time. John Marston was another, notable for a fierce line in satire. He had been at the receiving end of Jonson's latest satire in which he had been made to look no end of an idiot. The son of an English father and an Italian mother he seems to have inherited the worst of both nationalities, stubbornness and excitability. In *Histriomastix* he depicted the young Jonson in no very flattering terms. It is a wonder Jonson didn't call him out for a duel. Instead of that, and with merciful forbearance, he wrote *Cynthia's Revels* in which, trying to do better than merely score off a rival dramatist, he tried to ingratiate himself with the Queen. But all the same the caricatures were there. The answer came this time from Thomas Dekker, another ambitious young dramatist only a year older than Ben Jonson, who had also been the butt of Jonson's pen. Dekker's riposte came in a play called *Satiromastix*, but Jonson, always quick on the draw, got in first with *The Poetaster*. And there the matter ended.

This curious game of dramatic cut-and-thrust lasted from 1599 till 1601. The episode is known as the 'War of the Theatres'. The five plays to which it gave rise are miserably uneven, the work of ambitious and excitable young men, full of theories about dramatic art, critical of their society, and jealous of their professional reputations. And yet they are full of felicities. The very idea of *Every Man Out of His Humour*, which shows the bedevilment of a group of ridiculous characters, intended for contemporary types, all of whom cherish ambitions and affectations beyond their reach or alien to their nature, is a witty one and well suited to the satirical style of the play. *Cynthia's Revels* is slighter in construction, but one can't ignore a play that contains verses like this:

> *Queen and huntress, chaste and fair,*
> *Now the sun is laid to sleep,*
> *Seated in thy silver chair,*
> *State in wonted manner keep:*
> *Hesperus entreates thy light,*
> *Goddess, excellently bright.*

Let me leave Jonson for a moment to consider the condition of the theatre when it was possible for five full-length plays to be staged that fought out in public a private rivalry. Unfortunately we know none of the facts that would enable us to get our judgments right. We don't know the extent to which the three dramatists depended upon their plays for their livelihood, we don't know how many performances of each were given, nor with what success. Should one respect the Elizabethan play-going public for apparently showing such deep interest in the exuberance of their youngest dramatists? Or despise them for showing a contemptible concern over trivialities? Or is the answer that the manner in which the plays were written and staged brought far greater delight than we can appreciate today, the quality of the verse, the wit of the satire, the invention of the incidents, and the skill of the actors charming the Elizabethans as the only comparable play I can think of, *Love's Labour Lost*, charms us still today?

What we do know about the performance of these plays is that *Every Man Out of His Humour* was given by the Lord Chamberlain's Players and the remaining four by companies of boys. The popularity of these Boys' Companies is one of the extraordinary features of the Elizabethan theatre. Consider it together with the fact that boys played all the women's parts in the adult companies and one can only suppose that they were coached with a thoroughness that we can hardly conceive and in a style of acting which has been entirely lost.

It was a measure of the success of a company for it to receive an invitation to play before the Queen. Between 1558 and 1576 forty-six performances by boys and thirty-two by adults were given at court. Between 1576 and 1583 the popularity of the boys decreased. Between 1594 and 1603 twenty performances at court were given by adults and thirty-two by boys. It is astonishing to think that these companies of boys were perhaps even more popular with the public than Henslowe's company which in 1599 was playing Dekker's lovely play *The Shoemaker's Holiday* and Burbage's company which now had some of Shakespeare's masterpieces in its repertory, with Burbage himself playing the leading roles.

Now to return to Ben Jonson. It is evident that with the productions of *The Poetaster* and *Satiromastix* he had had his fill of this kind of controversy. Indeed it was not long before he and Marston became good friends and collaborated together with George Chapman in a breezy comedy of low-life called *Eastward Ho*. Perhaps the gloom and anxiety that settled upon the country with the death of Queen Elizabeth affected Jonson as it probably affected Shakespeare who at this time was writing his greatest tragedies. It was also at this time that Jonson became a Roman Catholic.

In 1604 Jonson's great tragedy *Sejanus* was produced by the Shakespeare-Burbage company, the idea having been suggested to Jonson perhaps by the success of Shakespeare's *Julius Caesar*. There exist considerable differences of opinion about the merits of this play. One critic of high standing has called it 'ponderously dull' and another says it is 'weighty and impressive'. For me it is exciting to read and by all reports—for I have not seen it myself—extremely effective upon the stage. It suffers in comparison with Shakespeare's play; none of his characters have the humanity of Brutus, Cassius, and Antony; but it is full of felicities, touches of character, strokes of wit, and splendid great speeches which make one long to hear them in the mouth of a fine actor. *Sejanus* and *Catiline* (1611) are not usually reckoned among Jonson's masterpieces but they stand honourably between the great plays he was about to write and the lesser plays he wrote at the beginning and end of his life.

It is clear, I think, that with *Sejanus,* Ben Jonson began to find the harmony of his creative personality, for he at once entered upon a great creative period, writing the masterpieces upon which his fame is based: *Volpone* (1605), *Epicoene,* often referred to by its sub-title *The Silent Woman* (1609), *The Alchemist* (1610), *Bartholomew Fair* (1614) and the re-written Londonified *Every Man in His Humour.* He becomes less possessed by antiquity and far more responsive to the London in which he lived and which was a far better source of inspiration. And yet his learning gives a kind of edge and glitter to his lines.

Let me give an example of this from his ebullient great farce *The Alchemist*. The play is the story of a monstrous impersonation. While the master of a London house is staying in the country on account of the plague his servant Jeremy sets up his friend Subtle as an alchemist and together they impose upon a strange collection of characters who come to them for help and advice; one to have his fortune told; Abel Drugger, who is to open a new shop, to know 'by the stars' how to arrange the shelves, where to put the doors, and so on; Sir Epicure Mammon to have his possessions turned to gold. Here is a part of a long speech in which Sir Epicure dreams of what he will do with his untold wealth :

> *I will have all my beds blown up, not stuft—*
> *Down is too hard: and then, mine oval room*
> *Filled with such pictures as Tiberius took*
> *From Elephantis, and dull Aretine*
> *But coldly imitated. Then, my glasses*
> *Cut in more subtle angles, to disperse*
> *And multiply the figures as I walk*
> *Naked between my succubae. My mists*
> *I'll have of perfume, vapour'd 'bout the room,*
> *To lose ourselves in; and my baths, like pits*
> *To fall into; from whence we will come forth*
> *And roll us dry in gossamer and roses.*

This leads me on to mention another important side of Jonson's genius. From his earliest plays he shows himself to have been a moralist. He was deeply concerned with people's behaviour; and the side of human nature that exasperated him most was the misuse of wealth. What an attack he makes upon it in *Volpone*! The opening of the play for instance, with Volpone leering over his piled hoards of treasure. Riches lead to every human virtue, he says to his servant Mosca, and continues:

> . . . Yet I glory
> More in the cunning purchase of my wealth
> Than in the glad possession, since I gain
> No common way; I use no trade, no venture;
> I wound no earth with ploughshares, fat no beasts
> To feed the shambles; have no mills for iron,
> Oil, corn, or men, to grind them into powder:
> I blow no subtle glass, expose no ships
> To threat'nings of the furrow-faced sea;
> I turn no monies in the public bank,
> No usurer private.

Can anyone miss the irony of these furious lines, spoken by a loathesome man who is entirely parasitical upon society—the dead contrary of what he says about himself —the man who buys gold in order that he may acquire more gold? Can anyone miss Jonson's grim humour as he gloats over this nauseating creature who has opened the play with the tremendous line:

> Good morning to the day, and next my gold !

I now want to give an example of Jonson's fun. *The Silent Woman* is another tremendous farce about a group of young scalliwags who impose upon an eccentric old miser to induce him to leave his money to his nephew. For sheer droll humour listen to this description of Morose, the miser, who can stand no noise.

Why sir, he hath chosen a street to lie in so narrow at both ends that it will receive no coaches, nor carts, nor any of these common noises.

XI
The interior of
the Globe

XII   Inigo Jones   XIII   Ben Jonson
XIV   John Dryden   XV   William Congreve

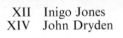

How does he for the bells? someone asks.

Oh in the Queen's time he was wont to go out of town every Saturday at ten o'clock, or on Holy day eves. But now, by reason of the sickness, the perpetuity of ringing has made him devise a room with double walls and treble ceilings; the windows close shut and caulked; and there he lives by candle-light. He turned away a man last week for having a new pair of shoes that creaked. And this fellow waits on him now in tennis-court socks, or slippers soled with wool; and they talk to each other in a trunk.

And when finally the deception is played on him, and he is married to a wife who never stops talking and the wedding is celebrated with drums and trumpets, in comes one of the characters hardly able to speak for laughter:

O hold me up a little, I shall go away in the jest else. He has got on his whole nest of nightcaps, and locked himself up in the top of the house, as high as ever he can climb from the noise. I peeped in at a cranny and saw him sitting over a cross-beam of the roof . . . upright: and he will sleep there.

And this is the dramatist who can drop into the middle of a play—it's *Cynthia's Revels*—a verse like this:

Slow, slow, fresh fount, keep time with my salt tears:
  Yet, slower, yet; O faintly, gentle springs:
List to the heavy part the music bears,
  Woe weeps out her division when she sings.
    Droop herbs and flowers,
    Fall grief and showers,
    Our beauties are not ours;
7

O, I could still,
Like melting snow upon some craggy hill,
Drop, drop, drop, drop,
Since nature's pride is now a wither'd daffodil.

I don't think that Jonson was under any doubt about his skill as a dramatist nor of his superiority to Shakespeare. I have already quoted his remark that Shakespeare 'never blotted out a line'. When he passed on this piece of information to his friend, William Drummond of Hawthornden, he added that 'he wished he had blotted out a thousand'. Jonson also contributed a Prologue of commendation to the *First Folio*. This famous remark seems to me to have an authentic ring: '. . . for I loved the man and do honour his memory (on this side idolatry as much as any).'

He sets out what he considers to be the reasons for his own superiority in a Prologue to the second version of *Every Man in His Humour*. As the syntax is not always clear and the poetry not of a high order, I will paraphrase it.

Many people have become poets through necessity, but he, Ben Jonson, is not so fond of the drama that he will seek for the approval of the public by indulging tricks which he dislikes: to show a child become a man, and grow old in a few hours; to portray the wars of York and Lancaster with a couple of rusty swords and some jog-trot verse; to smear on bloody scars in the dressing-room. This play is a model that others should follow. It has no chorus, no wooden throne, no bangs to frighten the women; no thunder in the form of iron balls rolled upon a wooden floor or drum beats to mark the height of the storm. This play is about recognizable men and women. It deals with human folly, not human crime; it is hoped the audience will laugh with the players not at them.

Jonson, you see, was a classicist. He had a highly developed sense of the fitness of things, of a play for its subject, of a scene for a play, of a word for a thought. But at the same time he was what we call a 'naturalist': he was inspired not by romantic fictional subjects but by the life of the people he saw around him in the streets of Westminster and the city of London. For these two reasons he despised the things for which the French have also hated the Elizabethans: their great sprawling plays, their disregard of time and place, their variety and complexity, their sensationalism, their storms and battles and murders and purple verse that made them so popular with the groundlings. He wrote plays of contemporary life but in the classical manner.

The reason, I think, why Jonson was able to free himself from any excessive clutter with classicism was that he had the opportunity to write a very large number of masques. The masque was a form of entertainment that had become extremely popular among the nobility of Tudor England. It is a difficult form of entertainment to describe for although it was very well suited to the tastes of the Renaissance princes with their love of music and dancing, of dressing-up and putting on a show, its origins are ancient. Some people believe the masque to be a kind of survival of the magical rituals which people performed to make the sun shine, the corn grow, and the people healthy. But by the time of Jonson the masque had become an elaborate and costly form of court entertainment in which some fanciful ideas were dressed up in allegorical form.

A very simple example of the way in which a masque was composed would go something like this. The masque, we will suppose, was to celebrate a notable wedding. It might well have opened with a scene of rocks and desolation, all rather romantically and attractively depicted, and peopled with witches and monstrous-headed animals. The movement and the singing would have been arranged with the greatest skill. Then some piece of scenery would have been rolled away revealing the God of Love who would drive away the witches and monsters and then, striking a particularly sombre rock, which would open, he would reveal the bridal pair; and a chorus of golden-headed youths and their ladies would enter singing to the effect that the world was a hideous place until it was made fair by the marriage of this particular couple. Performers and spectators would then join together in a bridal dance; and the whole thing would be full of references to characters and episodes appearing in the works of the old Greek and Roman authors.

It was particularly fortunate for Jonson that James I, who, you may remember, as James VI of Scotland had been invited to take the English crown on the death of Elizabeth, was a first-rate classical scholar, second in learning only to Jonson himself, and that his wife, Henrietta of Denmark, thought that every state occasion should be celebrated with a masque in which she could perform herself. The king's advisers realized quickly that of all the literary men in Jacobean England Jonson with his ebullient invention, exquisite gifts as a poet, and zest for classical quotation, was the man to write them. And when they roped in Inigo Jones to do the scenery they established one of the most famous collaborations in theatrical history. Of the thirty-seven surviving masques that were given at court or in the houses of the nobility between 1604 and 1631 twenty-two are by Jonson and in most of them he worked in collaboration with Inigo Jones. The uneasy partnership was eventually broken by a quarrel. In view of the irascibility of them both it is a wonder it lasted so long.

Let anyone with a real interest in this wayward genius dip into his masques and savour the facile charm of the lyrics, the inventiveness of the subjects, and the ease with which Jonson wears his learning, even when he is explaining every classical allusion in a footnote.

A famous episode in Jonson's life was his visit to the Scottish poet, Drummond of Hawthornden. Jonson, then aged forty-six, thinking he was getting too heavy, walked to Edinburgh, stayed three weeks with the poet, and then walked back to London. History fails to relate whether the effort lessened his circumference. In conversation with Drummond Jonson delivered himself of some fairly trenchant judgments on the poets and writers he had known. When he had left, Drummond formed his own shrewd opinion of his visitor and it seems to me that these few lines are probably a just estimation of this gifted irascible genius. And if Drummond fails to mention what interests us most, his dramatic works, that is probably because he had had little chance of reading them and none of seeing them performed on the stage.

He is a great lover and praiser of himself, a contemner and scorner of others, given rather to lose a friend than a jest, jealous of every word and action of those about him (especially after drink which is one of the elements in which he liveth) . . . thinketh nothing well but what either he him-

self or some of his friends and countrymen hath said or done.
He is passionately kind and angry, careless either to gain or
keep, vindictive, but if he be well answered at himself . . .
oppressed with fantasy which hath ever mastered his reason.
a general disease in many poets. His inventions are smooth
and easy but above all he excelleth in translation.

Of Jonson's long decline into old age, penury and incompetence I can only state the unhappy fact. He died in
1637 at the age of sixty-five. Let us remember him as the
author of four of the most splendid comedies in the
English language, some exquisite poetry, and as a memorable character.

SOME BOOKS FOR FURTHER READING:

That Jonson has for long been unpopular with critics and
scholars is evident in the poverty of the books that have been
written about him. John Palmer's *Ben Jonson* is a plain
account of the man, his work, and his life. Eric Linklater's
Ben Jonson and King James is anything but plain. It might
have been called *Don Juan in Elizabethan England*. The
mention of the King in the title is simply a gesture from one
Scot to another. Marchette Chute's *Ben Jonson of Westminster* is the most recent and satisfactory biography I have
found.

A selection of his plays is available in the Mermaid edition
(three volumes). There is a complete edition in Everyman
(two volumes) but the print is very small. Five of his best
plays are admirably printed in the World's Classics.

CHAPTER SEVEN

Dryden and Congreve

T HE FIRST DRAMATIST I shall write about in this chapter will be John Dryden. His first play was produced in 1663. This is little more than twenty years after the death of Ben Jonson. But during these twenty years England had divided herself into armed camps and fought a cruel civil war. The King had been executed and after an experiment in Republican government a new king had been invited to take the throne and the monarchy had been restored. This is not the place to discuss these tremendous events but they must not be taken for granted. The people of a country do not take up arms and fight pitched battles against each other, execute their king and establish a dictatorship, out of spite or boredom: they go to such extremes when their emotions allow of no other satisfaction. In the desperate years of the mid-seventeenth century England was not just enjoying a romantic adventure of Cavaliers and Roundheads, but fighting out the principles on which the country has been governed ever since.

I emphasize the immensity of the conflict that separates the theatre of Ben Jonson from that of John Dryden for several reasons. I do not think that outwardly the conditions of theatre-going were very different. The history of the theatre would show that in spite of the absolute prohibition of theatrical performances by the puritanical government of Cromwell and its methodical destruction of every one of London's six theatres, there is a fairly steady line of development. It had become customary for theatres to have roofs at least from the sixteen-twenties. Long before the Civil War James Shirley had begun to write the sort of plays that became enormously popular after the Restoration; and this was partly because the theatres were no longer supported by butcher and baker, nobleman and student, as the Globe and the Fortune had been, but by a rich and leisured class. Very profound changes which are explained in Economic Histories were transforming English society, and the emergence of this new class of people was one of its symptoms. They supported the theatres. The students stayed away. The theatres adapted themselves to their new clients. It always happens thus. A change in the country's economics creates a change in social groups, a change in people's habits and their tastes, and since theatres are dependent upon their audiences they are always liable to reflect a change rather than to initiate one.

So in spite of outward similarities there were enormous differences in spirit between London in the sixteen-thirties and the sixteen-sixties. And if the theatre is a true reflection of its audiences we might be inclined to imagine that Restoration England took its tone from Charles II, a gay sensual irresponsible fellow who dawdled through his reign sipping French wine and flirting with Nell Gwynne while his court indulged all the pleasures that had been denied the country for twenty years.

The truth of course is that the country didn't go through the agonies of the Civil War that it might surrender itself

to a decade of pleasure. We are speaking of the age of
Sir Isaac Newton, of Robert Boyle, and of the founding
of the Royal Society, among the objects of which was
the pious resolve that all technical works should be written
in decent English. It was also the age of the music of
Henry Purcell, of *Paradise Lost,* and of what the elderly
friend of my childhood, Henry Arthur Jones, used to call
'the flowering time of English prose'.

The tragedy for dramatic art was that it became
identified with a dead tradition. I mean by this that if
Marlowe had first come to London in 1663 I doubt
whether he would have written for the theatre. The giant
of English literature, John Milton, did write for the theatre
and the absolute failure as drama of *Samson Agonistes*
shows the beginning of the great divorce, that was to be
the downfall of the English drama, between the writers
and the theatre. I cannot but believe that if Milton had
been an Elizabethan he might have written tragic masterpieces to hold the stage with those of Shakespeare; and
that if Marlowe had lived at the time of the Restoration
he would have written epic poems.

One can see all this very clearly in the life of John
Dryden and it is for this reason that I have chosen to
write about him in preference to Sir George Etherege,
William Wycherley, Sir John Vanburgh or George
Farquhar, whose plays might be thought superior. But
Dryden I believe to be important for what he stood for
and for what he failed to do. He stands at the top of
the slippery slope down which the English drama proceeded to slither for two hundred years.

John Dryden was born in 1631 and educated at Westminster where, like Ben Jonson, he had plenty of rhetoric.

After a spell at Cambridge he became a clerk in the government service, writing poetry, as many a clerk had done before, in what little spare time he had. When he was offered accommodation in the house of a noble patron he accepted gladly; for it was the regular custom for wealthy noblemen to offer hospitality to needy artists.

At first he had little confidence in his powers or instinct for his own talents. In this he was quite different from Marlowe who sailed straight into the theatre with his guns blazing splendidly, and Ben Jonson who started off writing plays with vigour even though they were of the wrong kind.

But money was still not plentiful and odes in praise of Cromwell and then of Charles II brought him neither fame nor fortune. He looked around at what other opportunities there were for a literary genius and like Greene, Peele and Kyd before him, his eyes lighted on the theatre.

Unhappily the Restoration Theatre was no very meritorious affair. There were two theatres in London in 1661. One was administered by Sir William Davenant, a serious man who, by advancing the claims of the drama as something educational, had struggled throughout the Protectorate for permission to open a theatre. The other was in the hands of Sir Thomas Killigrew, a man of excellent good humour, a swaggerer, harsh of tongue, sharp in money matters and himself the author of a number of unsuccessful plays. He had spent part of his exile with Charles II trying to raise funds for his royal master. In 1662 he opened a newly-built theatre which stood very near the site of the present Drury Lane and is considered to be its ancestor.

Dryden's first attempts at playwriting were not success-

ful. But his third play, *The Wild Gallant,* was accepted by
Killigrew. Having no natural instinct for the theatre
Dryden did not try to achieve anything very original,
but wrote dutifully in the fashionable manner though
with little talent for it. Restoration Comedy has
come to be known as 'The Comedy of Manners' and by
1663, when *The Wild Gallant* was produced, Dryden cannot even have seen a first-rate example of its kind. He
was working in the twilight. He had neither a gift for the
sort of repartee that is the making of these plays nor an
inclination to move in the society where he might have
learnt it. On the contrary he was of a rather serious
disposition.

At the same time he was a scholar. He was familiar with
several foreign languages and he read widely. He rapidly
became familiar both with the English drama of the past
and the plays of other countries especially the French. He
read and he pondered, his lively critical faculties playing
upon everything that came beneath his attention. The
outcome of his reflections was a type of play to which he
gave the name, 'heroic tragedy'. It is in this connection that
Dryden becomes a dramatist to reckon with. These heroic
tragedies he came to consider his most important contribution to the drama.

I cannot urge people to read Dryden's plays, either his
comedies or his heroic plays, assured that they will find
as much pleasure in them as in those of Marlowe or
Jonson, and that in itself is a serious criticism. But it is
very well worth while making an effort at acquaintance-
ship. The best of the kind are *The Indian Emperor* (1665),
a play about Cortez and Montezuma in Mexico, *Almanazor
and Almahide* (1670-1), often referred to by its sub-title,

The Conquest of Granada, Aurung-zebe (1675), a curious play about India in the year 1660, and *All for Love* (1677).

John Dryden is rather like Bernard Shaw in that both of them left so many critical writings discussing their own as well as other people's work that we never need be in any doubt about their meaning and their methods. Dryden attached Prefaces and Dedications to most of his plays wherein he set forth a kind of apology for, or explanation of, the play that follows. Here we begin to see the reason for the assertion that John Dryden was the most conspicuous literary figure of the period apart from John Milton. He was in fact a magnificent critic, writing about his own plays as well as those of other dramatists with sharp perception and in admirable prose. When in 1666 the plague of London closed the theatres, he retired to the home of his father-in-law in Wiltshire and wrote his splendid *Essay of Dramatic Poesy* in which he sets forth his views on a large number of dramatic topics, and argues them from many different points of view.

The best way to understand Dryden's dramatic theories is to begin by reading his best serious play, *All for Love*. In this play he redramatizes the story of *Antony and Cleopatra* according to his own theories. He describes in the Preface how he has taken Shakespeare's fine but sprawling and ill-constructed tragedy, which he calls a 'chronicle-play', and reshaped it according to the ideals of heroic tragedy. This meant giving the play a unity of time, place, and action, for he had this in common with Ben Jonson (whom incidentally he very much admired, considering *The Silent Woman* to be a perfectly-constructed play) that he could not abide the utter disregard for time and place of the Elizabethans.

The theory of the dramatic unities is a pedantic business. In the seventeenth century it made many critics hot under the collar. Roughly speaking it came about like this. In Athens of the fifth century B.C. there were three great tragic dramatists, Aeschylus, Sophocles, and Euripides who wrote between them close on three hundred plays. In the following century a celebrated critic called Aristotle analysed these tragedies and pointed out that the best of them observed certain unities. The action was pressed into a limited space of time, and did not skip about excessively from place to place. Along came a lot of pedants in the fifteenth and sixteenth centuries, who were ready to make a Bible of anything said by the ancient Greeks, and insisted that a play observe these unities. Shakespeare must have been aware of the theory for it was propounded by Sir Philip Sidney, and we can imagine what Shakespeare thought of it. Dryden accepted the theory not because he was an obedient sort of fellow but because it seemed to him to be right and proper.

Although Dryden was a splendid poet it is very dangerous to compare him too closely with Shakespeare. In *Antony and Cleopatra* Shakespeare clearly intended to pull out every stop that might increase the passion, the colour, the excitement of the play, and his realization of these two tragic characters; and Shakespeare does not appear to have been at odds in any way with his audiences. But in *All for Love* Dryden was not trying to move people deeply according to the ideal of tragedy, but to present a tragic situation in the most elegant possible manner. He wanted to impose a certain discipline on Shakespeare and to dress this story in the fine-cut clothes of his period.

This process of refinement is best understood by the example of the French theatre. Throughout the seventeenth century the French writers and philosophers were deeply engaged in a tremendous attempt to understand the nature of man and to work out the correct behaviour for men and women in a civilized society. The stage, which *shows* manners as well as *talking* about them, came to play a leading part in this important experiment. The plays of Corneille are all about the duties and responsibilities of children to their parents, of citizens to their country, of Christians to their religion. The plays of Racine are about the nature of love, the extent to which it can and cannot be controlled, and of the violence of people's emotions when they are roused by love. Molière was a great satirist. He too was concerned with behaviour and seems to have thought that the manners which the French were so busily cultivating as necessary for civilized people led to artificiality, hypocrisy, and all kinds of stupidity and dishonesty. Many of the plays of Molière were translated into English.

Dryden claims that only certain stories and events are suitable as subjects for heroic plays and these are the subjects that have been treated in heroic poems such as the epics of Homer, Virgil, Ariosto, Tasso, and our English Spencer. Dryden also believed that while a heroic play gave considerable scope to a dramatist to indulge his powers of invention, its hero must be a man who is 'a perfect pattern of heroic virtue', that is, a perfect example of good behaviour.

Shakespeare, of course, and his fellow Elizabethans would have just laughed at the idea of standards of behaviour. Except perhaps Ben Jonson, whom Dryden followed in all sorts of ways. Jonson would have seen what Dryden was getting at.

The difference in aim and method between Shakespeare and Dryden can be seen by comparing the opening speeches of *Antony and Cleopatra* and *All for Love*. The passage from Shakespeare glows with the character of the man who is speaking. Dryden's poetry is more consciously elevated, more objective, less personal. We'll begin with Shakespeare.

A soldier is complaining about the behaviour of Antony who has been bewitched by the Egyptian Cleopatra.

> *Nay, but this dotage of our general's*
> *O'erflows the measure: those his goodly eyes,*
> *That o'er the files and musters of the war*
> *Have glow'd like plated Mars, now bend, now turn,*
> *The office and devotion of their view*
> *Upon a tawny front* [Cleopatra]: *his captain's heart,*
> *Which in the scuffles of great fights hath burst*
> *The buckles on his breast, reneges* [refuses] *all temper,*
> *And is become the bellows and the fan*
> *To cool a gipsy's lust.*

And here is a Priest of Isis speaking at the opening of Dryden's play:

> *Portents and prodigies have grown so frequent,*
> *That they have lost their name. Our fruitful Nile*
> *Flowed ere the wonted season, with a torrent*
> *So unexpected, and so wondrous fierce,*
> *That the wild deluge overtook the haste*
> *Even of the hinds that watched it: Men and beasts*
> *Were borne above the tops of trees, that grew*
> *On the utmost margin of the water-mark.*

Then, with so swift an ebb the flood drove backward,
It slipt from underneath the scaly herd:
Here monstrous phocae panted on the shore:
Forsaken dolphins there with their broad tails,
Lay lashing the departing waves: hard by them,
Sea horses floundering in the slimy mud,
Tossed up their heads, and dashed the ooze about them.

The comparison is not unfair to Dryden for his lines are splendid poetry. It is as drama I would ask you to consider them.

But I should also add that they are not typical of heroic drama for Dryden usually employed rhymed couplets, and, I think it must be agreed, with striking effect. Here are the opening lines of *The Conquest of Granada*:

Thus in the triumph of soft peace, I reign;
And from my walls defy the power of Spain;
With pomp and sports my love I celebrate,
While they keep distance and attend my state.

and so on for thousands of lines. Very stilted perhaps, and the enemies of Dryden were not slow to parody the style; but played by actors trained in the proper kind of declamation, and staged and dressed with the splendour of which the artists of that age were capable, these must have been impressive enough.

But how difficult it is to throw oneself back in imagination to the first production of a play! To know what it looked and sounded like and how the audience responded. One needs a lot of knowledge and a lot of imagination. As to the Restoration theatre we know that this was an age when people paid a great deal of attention to clarity and style in what they said and wrote; that it was the age of the music of Henry Lawes, of Henry Locke, and the divine Henry Purcell who devoted a large amount of his time to writing incidental music for the theatres. It was an age of the utmost splendour in fashion and there can be little doubt that the elegant costumes of the men and the rustling glowing silks and satins of the women must have looked extraordinarily magnificent in the light of the hundreds of candles with which the theatres of the time were lit. And since the theatres were small, and the auditoriums were not darkened during performances but were lit as brightly as the stage, the whole house must have presented a most lively spectacle.

'Lively' is almost certainly the word, for by every report the behaviour of audiences appears to have been execrable. Pepys and many other writers of the time have described the manner in which the audience used to chatter among themselves throughout the play, men argued and sometimes even fought, and orange-girls went around selling fruit throughout the performance. There were some who said that the audience provided better entertainment than the play. I cannot emphasize too strongly that from this time for well over a hundred years audiences behaved in a tyrannical manner, shouting down actors who didn't please them and demanding apologies of a player who showed resentment of this treatment. It was the audience that even decided whether to ' call ' an actor to take a bow.

Yet this was the audience for which John Dryden, classical scholar, Poet Laureate, critic of distinction, tragic dramatist, Catholic convert, wrote comedies over a stretch of thirty years. Is not that an extraordinary thing? But let us be quite clear about the details. Dryden perhaps couldn't help the audience. In *Marriage à la Mode* he certainly

8

didn't play down to them. But in a number of other comedies, a preposterous piece called *Limberham* for instance, he outdoes the filthiest of his colleagues. But it's not the filth that seems to me to matter; it's the ineptitude of the play, the tediousness of it; and yet this tremendous poet can publish this play with a sycophantic dedication to some noble lord in which he claims that it is among his finest works!

The usual defence of writers of this kind, and it was used by all the Restoration dramatists when they were attacked, is that they are depicting the vices of the age in order to show them up to ridicule. A very pretty casuistry. For it would be extremely difficult to prove that a satirical play has ever reformed anything for all the assertions of the satirists. If it is a good play people are far too engrossed enjoying a vigorous piece of theatrical entertainment, and a moving emotional experience perhaps, to apply the lesson to themselves. I think it far more likely that a performance will impress upon the audience a certain sympathy for the situations the dramatist has intended to satirize.

But this is a difficult subject which has perplexed many thoughtful people. Restoration comedy is a sort of perpetual challenge to our moral standards. If we applaud, we're as bad as the people in the play. If we protest, we're whited sepulchres. My own complaint is a simple one. It is simply that one does not feel that a moment in the conscience of Restoration England is embedded in these plays as it is embedded in many an Elizabethan play. If anything is embedded it is the domination of dishonesty between the sexes; and though this may have been true of the theatregoing public it wasn't true of Restoration England.

In any case the policy didn't pay great dividends and the history of the two theatres is a lamentable tale of unsuccessful enterprises, only redeemed by the stature and worth of the great actor-manager Thomas Betterton. But the tale takes a turn for the better with the arrival in London of the gay young William Congreve, witty, and most important of all, with the manuscript of a masterpiece in his pocket. The various authorities I have consulted tell conflicting tales about the meeting of Congreve with Dryden. Some say that it was at the stage door of Drury Lane, some that it was at a local coffee shop. The upshot was that Congreve gave the manuscript of his play, *The Old Bachelor* to Dryden who was then becoming the Grand Old Man of English literature. Dryden was then connected with Drury Lane Theatre; he recognized the quality of the play and took it away to make some improvements. This began a close friendship between the two men which lasted till the death of Dryden eight years later.

The Old Bachelor was produced in 1693. In the two following years Congreve wrote and saw produced two more masterpieces, *The Double-Dealer* and the magnificent *Love for Love*. Since Betterton produced both these plays, one at Drury Lane and the other at his new theatre in Lincoln's Inn Fields, and since the ladies in his company were particularly skilful, both plays must have received splendid performances.

So by 1695 Congreve, still only twenty-five, was at the very height of his success. Two years later he wrote a piece of conventional Restoration tragedy, *The Mourning Bride*. In 1700 he produced the play which most people consider his masterpiece, *The Way of the World*.

With Congreve we are dealing with one of the absolute

masters of English comedy. Congreve, when attacked for his improprieties, asserted roundly that he was a satirist and that the refinement of manners and of behaviour was his aim. Well . . . read his plays and decide for yourself whether he wrote *Love for Love* as a protest at people's behaviour or for the joy of inventing such a gallery of amusing characters. At any rate the lords and ladies of London laughed their heads off at his plays and invited the brilliant young author to their parties. This suited Congreve down to the ground. He loved nothing better than the company of what is known as 'high society' and he was never so happy as when he had an audience round him provoking him to further brilliant sallies and laughing loudly at his wit.

But he also wanted to be a great dramatist. At first he was able to keep his social and his professional life in proper proportion. Each play was better than the last. Society gave him the material and adored to see its imperfections so brilliantly dramatized, refined, shaped into miracles of delicate construction, and heightened by a dialogue that in its poise, its levity, its wit has never been surpassed. All the metaphors that suggest steel and sparkle, brilliance and dazzle that have been applied to Congreve's comedies are justified. Congreve perfectly succeeded in what he set himself to do.

But the story ends in tragedy. In 1700, the year of the first production of *The Way of the World*, Dryden died. Though Congreve lived another twenty-nine years he did not write a single further play. Of course there were reasons for this collapse. His health was bad. He had wined and dined too much. He was worsted in a literary quarrel with one Jeremy Collier. And *The Way of the*

World was a failure with the public. A man of spirit, only thirty years of age, might have lived through such difficulties and recaptured the creative spirit; but only, I think, in congenial circumstances. And this is the place to remember that the theatre had forfeited its integrity long since.

Dryden and Congreve are known to have spent long hours in the coffee-shop together, one in his declining years, the other prematurely old. Perhaps they discussed, perhaps they sat meditating the attack that had been made upon them, and upon Congreve especially, by a high-church controversialist, this Jeremy Collier, in a pamphlet called *A Short View of the Profaneness and Immorality of the English Stage*. As a matter of fact the pamphlet is not particularly short. Jeremy Collier's attack is comprehensive in scope and very accurately aimed. Twenty years before, Dryden would have plunged into such a controversy with relish; but he had now expressed his shame for his licentious comedies. Congreve composed an answer and Collier's answer to the answer was more damning than the original attack.

I do not suppose for a moment that these two great writers as they sat and mused in their coffee-shop realized that the tide was against them. They cannot have known that the new century was to be called by the philosophers the 'Age of Enlightenment'; but they must have realized that if the theatre was to be taken seriously, it had to take itself seriously, and think out afresh its nature and responsibilities. This is what Dryden had tried to do and that is why I am disposed to honour him. Unfortunately heroic tragedy was dead. It had never been particularly vigorous. The Comedy of Bad Manners, as it has not very wittily been called, had been shamed out of existence by Jeremy Collier and yawned from the stages by a new generation of theatre-goers whose tastes were different. The alternatives? No one faced them squarely. The British drama sped headlong down the slope at the bottom of which lay Kemble's production of *Blue Beard* with twenty elephants.

SOME BOOKS FOR FURTHER READING:

There are good books about the history of this interesting but difficult period. Here are some. John Palmer's *The Comedy of Manners,* Bonamy Dobrée's *Restoration Comedy* and *Restoration Tragedy,* Allardyce Nicoll's *A History of English Drama,* Volume I. On the Restoration Theatre there are Montague Summers's *The Restoration Theatre* and *The Theatre of Pepys,* and W. MacQueen Pope's *Theatre Royal, Drury Lane.* Biographies are: David Nichol-Smith's *John Dryden* (very short), T. S. Eliot's *Homage to John Dryden,* Kenneth Young's *John Dryden* (great fun), and Sir Edmund Gosse's *Life of William Congreve* (extraordinary that this interesting and brilliant man should not have been the subject of a more recent work).

The best or complete works of all the Restoration dramatists are included in the Mermaid series. Both Everyman and the World's Classics publish complete editions of Congreve and also anthologies of Restoration Tragedies and Comedies. By the Restoration dramatists I mean Etherege, Wycherley, Vanburgh, Otway and Farquhar as well as Dryden and Congreve. There are others less celebrated discussed in the books I have recommended.

CHAPTER EIGHT

Richard Sheridan

S HERIDAN WROTE THE happiest comedies in the English
language. I cannot imagine anyone who enjoys going
to the theatre failing to snort and guffaw at almost any
of them. And having said that it's really captious to be
critical. What Sheridan set out to do, which was to make
people laugh, to supply first-rate theatrical entertainment,
he perfectly succeeded in. If higher criticism says that he
lacked orginality, that he lifted his plots and his situations
from other lesser plays, it's saying only what Shakespeare
did and many another great writer. Originality of material
has never been a feature of dramatists until recent times :
it's the treatment that counts, the use the dramatist makes
of his material.

If one becomes more critical still and criticizes Sheridan
for the shallowness of his plays and the artificiality of
their situations that is only to commit what seems to me
the grave offence of criticizing a man for not having done
what he never set out to do.

Richard Sheridan was not a great artistic personality.
He neither saw deeply, thought deeply, nor felt deeply.
He was witty, alert, adroit, gracious, in fact he was a
thoroughly civilized and in many ways a brilliant man,
but he was not a world-shaker as Shakespeare was or even
a theatre-shaker as Dryden barely failed to be.

He had the misfortune to live in a century when the theatre had lost all contact with literature, with thought, with the problems of life, even on the most domestic level. No single aspect of the national consciousness erupted into the drama of the eighteenth century except as a cloudy mixture of sentimentality, windy passion, and rather feeble humour.

During the eighteenth century the London theatres were kept open not by the quality and interest of the plays but by musicians and actors. In the early years of the century some of the most successful theatrical performances had been those of Handel's exquisite operas, most of which were staged at Vanburgh's Theatre in the Haymarket, opposite the site of the present Haymarket Theatre. These were succeeded by a great vogue for ballad operas, as they were called, of which the first was that jolly piece *The Beggar's Opera* which is not an opera at all. These ballad operas were really plays with music. That's to say they had lively stories, plenty of dialogue, and a song based on a ballad or folk-song every few minutes. All kinds of musical entertainments were given in the London theatres with great success throughout the eighteenth century. Even Shakespeare was done to music. A famous production of *Macbeth* was advertised as having a chorus of singing witches.

But the eighteenth century was also the age of some very great English actors, and I am inclined to believe that if it hadn't been for Thomas Betterton at the beginning of the century, David Garrick in the middle, and John Philip Kemble, together with his sister Sarah Siddons, in the last decades, the theatre would have descended into an even worse plight than in fact it did.

It is very difficult for an actor, who is bound to the plays that are available for him to act, to be an innovator or leader in the theatre. But Betterton, Garrick and Kemble were different from most stars of the nineteen-fifties in that they were also theatre-managers. So by the administration of their companies they were able to impose a certain policy upon the theatre. Betterton, who lived throughout the difficult years of the period that I covered in the last chapter, deserves the infinite thanks of posterity for preserving professional standards, gathering round him a group of admirable players, and reviving the plays of Shakespeare and the Elizabethans when new plays of sufficient quality were not forthcoming.

Garrick, who introduced a number of technical innovations into the theatre, was another actor-manager who compelled the serious attention of the critics. Great drama has continually produced great acting but great acting does not appear to attract dramatists.

Thus when Sheridan came to London in 1773 he found adequate and sometimes brilliant acting in the leading theatres, a mixed collection of plays, and a public which was not without its standards of critical appreciation. The situation was not as bad as it might have been.

The important facts about Sheridan's early life have been neatly summarized by Leigh Hunt:

The Sheridans (were a family) in which intellect has been hereditary; for Dr Sheridan, the grandfather, though he preferred his jest and his fiddle, and his stockings down-at-heel, to a more solid reputation and prosperity . . . was a really learned and able man. The father (the actor and elocutionist) was a man of abilities also, in spite of his pedantry . . . and what he wanted towards augmenting the intellectual celebrity of his race was abundantly supplied by his wife. Their son was the author of *The Rivals* and *The School for Scandal*. He married a charmer for beauty and song.

Richard Sheridan was born in Dublin in 1751 and educated at Harrow. (How valuable a strain of the Kelt appears to be in a dramatist!) In 1770 the family moved to Bath, where father, Thomas Sheridan, settled down to teach elocution to the fashionable beaux of that most fashionable town. The young Sheridan, now nineteen, was at a loose end. The devil finding work for idle hands, he got himself involved in a somewhat complicated but highly romantic scrape with a young lady called Elizabeth Linley (the charmer for beauty and song). She was in fact well-known as a beauty and as a singer. This Miss Linley had become 'involved' with a man for whom she had little regard and decided that her only possible escape was in fleeing to the continent. Sheridan accompanied her, and having seen her safely established in Lille he returned to England, and fought a couple of duels with the young lady's persecutor in the second of which he was some-what worsted. Both fathers were opposed to further friendship between Richard and Elizabeth. Father Sheridan sent his son away to study law and father Linley quite simply forbade his daughter to become engaged to a young man without money or prospects.

Less than nine months later Richard Sheridan and Elizabeth Linley were married. So much for the opposition of parents.

After a honeymoon—all this taking place in 1773—the Sheridans set up house in London and since Sheridan had no money of his own and refused to live on the considerable income his wife might have made as a singer, had he allowed her, which he didn't, they were extremely poor.

For a year he wrote poems, political pamphlets. . . . Like Dryden before him he took time to know himself and to realize where his talents lay. Like Dryden, Congreve, and many another young writer he eventually wrote a play because he saw it as a possible source of fame and fortune.

The play was *The Rivals* and the story of its initial failure and ultimate success is a testimony to all concerned. On January 17th the play opened at Covent Garden. It was a failure. The audience was simply not amused. Sheridan immediately re-wrote it. Some of the actors were changed. It was rehearsed again and the new version was presented on January 28th, a fortnight later. It was a great success and has taken its place as one of the great comedies of the English language.

On May 2nd his second play, *St Patrick's Day or The Scheming Lieutenant*, was staged with moderate success. This would now be called a 'pot-boiler' and does not rate among Sheridan's notable achievements.

He then turned his hand to writing the libretto for a light opera, a form of entertainment which, as I have said, had been popular in London since the production of *The Beggar's Opera* in 1728. Father Linley helped to provide the music but does not seem to have entered into the spirit of the thing with much enthusiasm and col-laborated only because he realized the necessity of getting the young couple supplied with money.

The Duenna was staged on November 21st, 1775. It was an enormous success. Critics rated it far more highly than we do today.

The episode that follows seems to me to present an extraordinary and unexpected side to Sheridan's character. David Garrick who had been manager of Drury Lane Theatre since 1747 and was now nearing sixty, announced his retirement. Sheridan decided to buy Garrick's rights in the theatre himself, an incredible decision. Garrick wanted the stupendous figure of £35,000, a sum that must be counted in terms of several hundred thousand pounds according to the present value of money. With brilliant skill and perseverance Sheridan raised a third of the money himself and the rest from father-in-law Linley and a fashionable physician by the name of Dr James Ford. An elaborate arrangement of mortgages was involved and Sheridan conducted the whole affair with a remarkable understanding of high finance.

One can't help wondering what it was all about. It seems at first sight an extraordinary thing that a young man who had the utmost apparent faculty for writing brilliant and successful comedies should have saddled himself with the responsibility of running an enormous theatre—for Drury Lane was enormously bigger than the intimate playhouse of Restoration times; and it is even more startling perhaps that three years later and without surrendering his interest in the theatre, he should have gone into politics. By every report Sheridan was a gentle Irishman with blue eyes, a charming smile, a witty tongue, and a beautiful wife. Was he restless then like a child who is unable to settle at anything? Or brilliantly irresponsible? Was he really not satisfied writing plays? He must have known that when he undertook the management of Drury Lane he was going to make it increasingly difficult ever to find time to write. He cannot have believed in some kind of private myth of his own incredible fertility, for he knew better than anyone that he did not write easily. Those facile plays that seem to flow from the pen were the result of many long tormented hours at his writing-table. Did he then recognize that his talent was a limited one, too dependent upon second-hand material for him to be able to envisage a lifetime of professional playwriting?

The answer to these questions is very simple and extremely interesting. Sheridan was an ambitous man though I don't think he let many people realize it. It was hidden behind an impression of reticence. He liked to let people think he was a lazy fellow. Yet he was far more ambitious than Congreve, for instance, who had been content to make the ladies swoon. He wanted to be Somebody in the world. He might even have had his eye on politics from the start. And he must have realized that most people held so low an opinion of the theatre that no one would ever think much of a man whose only claim to distinction was as a writer of amusing plays. But to be manager of Drury Lane, that was to begin to cut a figure in the world; and for all the financial anxieties involved, it would be the source of a fluctuating but steady income.

So he now faced the tremendous task of finding new plays and judging the public taste with sufficient discernment to be able to choose old ones ready for revival. He got busy himself; revived *The Rivals*; re-wrote one of Vanburgh's wittiest and most indecent plays, *The Relapse*, and brought it out under the title of *A Trip to Scarborough*; but the public would have none of it.

He was saved from disaster by the success of his own masterpiece, *The School for Scandal*. Never can actors have awaited a new play with greater anxiety and impatience. Sheridan wrote slowly and carefully. As he completed each scene it was put into rehearsal under the direction of David Garrick. After being very nearly banned by the Lord Chamberlain the night before it was due to open, the play was presented with a brilliant company on May 8th, 1777. Playgoers of the time testified that the roars of applause greeting the curtain of the fourth and fifth acts were greater than anything that had been heard in the theatre in their lifetime.

The next day one of the morning papers had this to say about the performance:

Yesterday morning Mrs Sheridan was delivered of a son. The mother and child are likely to do well. In the evening of the same day Mr Sheridan's muse was delivered of a bantling which is likely to live for ever.

It was not for another two years, October 1779, that Sheridan's next play was staged. *The Critic,* once again, was a great success. Judging by its enormous popularity today, it is not difficult to understand that in 1779, when the theatrical conventions it burlesques and the notabilities it satirizes were in everybody's minds, it must have been a most dazzling experience to see it.

It is from this moment that the career of Sheridan begins to take a curious course. He wrote little more for the theatre. His remaining dramatic works, spread over many years, include a couple of pantomimes and a *Harlequinade* that are lost, and an heroic melodrama of the kind which he satirized so wittily in *The Critic.* That *Pizarro,* played with a splendid cast that included John

Philip Kemble, his son Charles, and his sister Sarah Siddons should have been a great success underlines the wretched dramatic standards of the day. I suppose it is true to say that gushing sentimentality, easy patriotism, mock heroism, and violent melodrama, are important ingredients of dramatic art, for they are human emotions at their most unrestrained. But here we leave the world of the Masters of the Drama for the so-called popular drama on which I have no brief to write. For what signifies the master is not, as I have said, his ability to stick to the rules, but to take basic human thoughts and feelings and by means of his literary and dramatic skill to express and interpret them by showing living people responding to and living under the stress of these emotions. And who does not find the emotional verbiage of *Pizarro* a little sickening after the glorious wit, urbanity, and civilized qualities of *The School for Scandal*?

After the production of *The Critic* Sheridan entered politics as Member of Parliament for Stafford. He led an active political life until 1812 and delivered his quota of brilliant speeches.

His continued management of Drury Lane belongs to the history of the theatre rather than of drama but I shall permit myself a paragraph for the sorrow of telling the lamentable tale.

In 1791 Drury Lane had fallen into such a state of disrepair that he was obliged to pull much of it down and rebuild it. The new building had the colossal capacity of 3,611 spectators. In 1808 Covent Garden was destroyed by fire. In February 1809 Drury Lane was destroyed by fire. Sheridan was in the House of Commons where members were debating the war in Spain. When news of the conflagration was known the Speaker proposed adjourning the House. Sheridan, who was thought to be a little drunk at the time, rose and said that 'whatever might be the extent of his private calamity he hoped it would not interfere with the public business of the country'. He left the House and betook himself to a coffee-shop near the burning theatre where he ordered a bottle of wine. It is reported, by whom I have never been able to discover, that when a friend remarked upon his calmness he replied, 'Cannot a man take a glass of wine by his own fireside?'

His career ended like the career of too many of the men who have been discussed in this book. His political career declined. He lost his seat in Parliament. He was often drunk. In 1813 he was arrested and imprisoned for debt. He passed the last years of his life in obscurity and dotage, cadging a glass of brandy and water from his friends. Jonson, Wycherley, Congreve, and now Sheridan, men who before they were forty had written great plays, imperishable masterpieces. . . . One might almost think it the nature of dramatic art to extract such brilliant talents from young men and then leave them worthless and exhausted to endure a protracted and imbecile old age. I do not think it is dramatic art as such that is to blame : it was the conditions that existed in the theatre for two hundred and fifty years, the conditions that divorced the theatre from the main stream of thought and literature and gave it a tradition for emotional vagabondage.

But conditions are made by men, submitted to by men, and changed by men. Marlowe, Jonson, Shaw and O'Casey tried to change them. Congreve, Sheridan and Pinero submitted.

XVI
The screen
scene from
*The School for
Scandal*

XVIII Drury Lane destroyed by fire

XVII Sheridan's Drury Lane Theatre

SOME BOOKS FOR FURTHER READING:

The most accessible biographies are: Walter Sichel's *Sheridan* (two heavy volumes of it), Lewis Gibbs's *Sheridan* (good plain fare), and W. A. Darlington's *Sheridan* (short and brightly written and with most of the essential material).

Editions of his plays are so plentiful that I need not specify them.

CHAPTER NINE

Arthur Pinero

SIR ARTHUR WING PINERO (1855-1934) is by no means everybody's pleasure. He wrote some thirty plays and although some of the best have appeared in anthologies and collections they have not been reprinted in a collected edition since they first appeared. They are rarely revived for, like a large number of other plays written fifteen years either side of 1900, they await the creation of a National Theatre to keep them before the public. Some people may question Pinero's right to be considered alongside Jonson, Sheridan, and Shaw. He is not to be compared with Tom Robertson, who wrote some twenty years earlier, as an innovator, he is not as witty as Oscar Wilde, his contemporary, and he is not so thoughtful as Granville Barker, whose output was much smaller. Others may simply find more to praise in the work of John Galsworthy, Sir James Barrie, or Somerset Maugham. Let me then try to justify the inclusion of Pinero in this book.

To begin with, Pinero has an important historical position in the theatre and it came about like this.

Drury Lane under the management of Sheridan, together with the other London theatres, made mock of the English drama. John Philip Kemble at least tried to keep Shakespeare in front of the public but we find Leigh Hunt protesting (in 1811) at Kemble having introduced twenty horses into a melodrama. Performances became longer, sometimes being composed of four different plays, ballets, harlequinades or musical pieces. The theatres were enormous and extremely uncomfortable. The audience sat on hard benches, and during the intervals women with huge and clumsy baskets came round selling fruit and bottles of stout which they offered to the public in loud shrill voices. Not even a splendid succession of actors could stem the tide of debasement. Kemble was followed by Kean and Kean by Macready but they were exceptions in a widespread impoverishment of the drama.

I have continually complained of the divorce between the theatre and the literature of the country. Those who have followed their English literature will remember that at the beginning of the nineteenth century there was a literary movement known as the 'Romantic Revival'. It was associated with one of the most splendid outbursts of lyric poetry in the language. And the extraordinary fact is that while every single one of the romantic poets had a shot at writing plays, none of them succeeded in writing an actable one: Byron, Coleridge, Scott, Shelley, Keats, Landor, Beddoes, Tennyson, Arnold, and Swinburne all failed. Shelley with *The Cenci* and Tennyson with *Harold* and *Beckett* were the only ones to approach success. Yet one's only got to read Byron's *Cain* or Browning's *Dramatis Personae* to realize that the spirit of romanticism was intensely dramatic. The romantic poets had the passion, the mastery of language, the interest in human beings, particularly those inspired with a great ideal, which are the essential qualities of a dramatist . . . and yet they failed. They did so, I am inclined to think, because the various elements that go to make up a successful theatrical performance had lost touch with each other. The theatres were too big for any drama, the audiences had no critical standards, and the writers for all their genius wrote nothing more than romantic poems in dramatic form. They had lost that grip upon the real essence and quality of the theatre.

Leigh Hunt, in an interesting passage written in 1831, discusses what he calls 'the supposed decline in the taste for drama' and attributes it to the lessening interest of the middle classes through the decline of smoking; for instead of passing the evenings in taverns or attending other amusements of town life such as the theatre, people had begun to stay at home and pass the time in reading, music, and visiting friends. Their place in the theatres had been taken by the uneducated classes who were profiting, he says, 'from the diffusion of knowledge'. This at least is an original point of view and whether or not he was right about smoking, we would agree, I think, about the change in the composition of the audiences. In fact it took another economic revolution to reform the theatre.

A renewed harmony between theatres, theatre-managers, actors, dramatists, and their public was not created until the eighteen-sixties. Sir Squire Bancroft and Marie Wilton, who subsequently became his wife, responded to a kind of instinct—the sure mark of a real showman of which everyone in the theatre needs a streak—that there might be a public ready to pay a high price for a seat in a small comfortable theatre presenting intelligent well-acted plays.

Squire Bancroft built his theatre—on the site of the present Scala—equipped the stalls with comfortable blue seats with lace antimacassars, charged ten shillings and sixpence a seat, and staged a number of plays by a young stage-manager called Tom Robertson, which are models of wit, charm, sentiment and honest bourgeois entertainment. Bancroft thereby secured the support of the Victorian middle-classes not so much for the theatre, for they had already supported the spectacular productions of Charles Kean, but for a revolutionary kind of drama which we now call 'naturalistic'. It was a prose drama, it was far more closely related to the interests of ordinary people than the romantic drama had been, and it was staged in as naturalistic a manner as their technical resources permitted them. (The use of electric light in the eighteen-eighties enormously increased the opportunities for naturalistic effects.)

Another great change took place in theatre-management. A manager like Sheridan had financed his theatre out of his own resources, depending entirely on receipts from the sale of tickets. If he needed a large sum to repair his theatre he had to borrow it on some security. But during the nineteenth century the cost of staging a play rose considerably. Far more trouble was taken with the production and far more money was spent on it. The Repertory system, which I described in the opening chapter, was now completely dropped and managements had no more interest in maintaining a permanent company. The production of each play became a separate financial undertaking, and it was expected to run for many hundreds of performances. At the same time—I am speaking of the second half of the nineteenth century—many new theatres were built and came under the control of commercial managements, very different in their attitude from the old actor-managers who were now on the way out. The theatre was therefore transformed into an industry with capital and shareholders and all the other unpleasant financial complications of a big industry—only this was the industry of entertainment, or 'show business' as the Americans came to call it.

Sir Arthur Pinero was the first outstanding dramatist of the commercialized theatre.

He climbed to eminence on the shoulders of a number of other dramatists whose names are to be found in any history of the drama; his name is continually coupled with that of Henry Arthur Jones who is in some ways a more interesting as he was certainly a more enterprising dramatist. But for sheer professional competence in the craft of play writing there was no one to touch him.

To understand the work of some dramatists it is helpful to know something about the sort of men they were and the theatre they worked for. Not in the case of Pinero. Pinero is inseparable from his plays. He did nothing of note in his life—except write plays. He wasn't a 'character' of whom people told endless anecdotes as they do of Oscar Wilde and Winston Churchill. Yet for nearly twenty years he was what Hesketh Pearson calls 'the playwright-autocrat of the English theatre'.

He spent the first ten professional years of his life as an actor, for that is the best way of learning the job. His first successes came when he was in the early thirties with a group of farces he wrote for the management of the Royal Court Theatre in Sloane Square. The names of these farces are *The Magistrate* (1885), *The Schoolmistress* (1886), and *Dandy Dick* (1887). These plays put him among the most successful playwrights of his day and they are still an admirable introduction to his work. Turn to them without delay for they are among the few plays I know that make people laugh aloud in the reading. The reason for this lies not in their wit but in their immaculate construction. Pinero begins with an admittedly farcical situation, and wrings from it the richest humour without ever running the joke to death like poorer dramatists who repeat without developing their situations.

Next to be enjoyed are two splendid comedies, *Trelawney of the Wells* (1898) and *The Gay Lord Quex* (1899). I hope that the former play at any rate will hold a place in the repertory of English comedy for many years. It has nothing approaching the pungency of *The Alchemist*, the wit of *Love for Love* or the situations of *The School for Scandal*, but it is intensely warmhearted, rich in the humour of character, and a lovely apostrophe to the theatrical profession itself. The story is based on the early years of Tom Robertson who like Pinero himself was an actor until he won success as a playwright.

But it is on his social dramas that Pinero's reputation will ultimately rest, a group of plays which he wrote with so deliberate a technique that I must introduce them with a few words about his dramatic methods.

The plots of Pinero's farces are intensely 'contrived', and I am bound to say that I do not use this word in an altogether complimentary sense. The long arm of coincidence is very long, and one cannot help feeling that people turn up far too often at conveniently the wrong moment for credibility. Pinero might well have answered that in his farces at any rate he was not trying to be credible but funny. His success is not in question. But

if our credibility is strained too far our amusement
diminishes.

Now Pinero probably took more trouble with the construction of his plays than any other dramatist to be
mentioned in this book though others have laboured long
over composition. He constructed his plays according to a
deliberate pattern, beginning with a situation that involved
a group of people in some striking relationship to each
other, developing it by means of subtle interplay between
the characters and the careful invention of fresh material
to some dramatic or hilarious denouement shortly before
the end of the play, and rounding it off with a final act
in which the complications and entanglements are
straightened out as naturally as possible.

Some critics in Pinero's day, as Bernard Shaw for
example, became highly critical of what came to be called
the 'well-made' play on the grounds that a story so in-
geniously constructed was bound to present a contrived
and unrealistic view of life. Pinero might have answered
that he was not interested in giving a naturalistic repre-
sentation of real life but in writing a play. A play was a
form of art and therefore essentially unnatural. His job
was to take a situation from real life, the more amusing
or poignant the better, and to develop it in such a way
as to create an effective piece of theatrical craftsmanship.
May I remind you that this craftsmanship is extremely
well discussed in the brilliant books by William Archer
and G. P. Baker which I recommended at the end of the
first chapter.

Pinero's first serious play was produced in 1889. It
was called *The Profligate*. Anyone wishing to follow the
development of Pinero should read this play but hesitate

to judge him by it. He did much better. Here are the dates and titles of the serious dramas by which, I imagine, he would hope to be remembered:

1893	*The Second Mrs Tanqueray*
1895	*The Notorious Mrs Ebbsmith*
	The Benefit of the Doubt
1901	*Iris*
	Letty
1906	*His House in Order*
1908	*The Thunderbolt*
1909	*Mid-Channel*

They really are extraordinarily impressive, these massive plays with their powerful stories and highly dramatic situations, and just as I find the farces irresistibly amusing, so I find these serious pieces the sort of plays that keep me reading long after I ought to be asleep.

This is a tremendous testimony to the skill of the telling for Pinero has a negligible imaginative range, very limited outlook and interests, and draws his characters almost wholly from the well-to-do class of late-Victorian and Edwardian London. The men are wealthy bankers, stock-brokers, or men-of-means who have no need of a job. Each has his own butler and more clothes in his wardrobe than many of us today will own in a lifetime. The women are always beautiful, usually pampered, generally unhappy. They are waited upon by maidservants in palatial houses in Mayfair or overlooking Lake Como. One sometimes feels that the whole lot would be the better for a day's hard digging in the garden.

Now as to what they are about. *The Second Mrs*

Tanqueray is about a woman, Paula, who once lived a dishonest and immoral kind of existence, mixing amongst men without proper regard for the status of married life. She was what was called in those days 'a scarlet woman'. You've undoubtedly seen the type on the films. The play tells of Paula's marriage to Aubrey Tanqueray, a highly respectable young man, and her failure to live down, or to persuade Aubrey's friends to let her live down, her past life.

Iris shows the tragic conflict of a wealthy woman who has to choose between a luxurious and pampered life as the wife or mistress of a wealthy but unattractive business man and a life of poverty in a log-cabin in Canada with a rather dull, square-jawed young Englishman.

Mid-Channel is about a wealthy stockbroker and his spoilt, pampered wife who after being married for fourteen years begin to drift apart, seek for fresh experiences, and end by destroying each other. Indeed, there is so little difference between one of Pinero's pampered spoilt heroines and another that when the other day for the purpose of this essay I re-read most of his plays I had the greatest difficulty in recalling one from another only a day or two afterwards.

Pinero's tragic theme is the destruction of individuals by their failure to comply with the social code. This code, in Victorian and Edwardian society, was a Mosaic law. Be clear that I am not speaking about the laws of England which prescribe certain penalties for married couples who break their marriage vows. In the plays of Pinero it is not the arm of the law that falls upon the hapless couples who fall out with each other but the massive weight of Victorian middle-class opinion, unspoken but accepted by all. You can call this opinion prejudice, but it remains just as cruel and evil a thing. Such a rigid moral atmosphere is so hard for us to understand these days—though I hasten to say that I do not think we are any greater sinners—that I can only explain it by saying that the first ambition of many ambitious men and idle acquisitive women was to get 'accepted' by high society. They then became members of certain clubs, watched cricket from the Pavilion at Lords, dined with certain people who were also fortunate enough to have been accepted, and sat in the stalls at the first performance of every new play by Sir Arthur Wing Pinero. But if a man became too friendly with another man's wife, or cheated at cards, or wore the wrong clothes at Hurlingham, or went around with an attractive young lady who was known to have once been a dancer in a Paris night club, he was not only ostracized and pitched out of society, but spiritually destroyed. The plays of Pinero show us how this happened.

The play in which we can see the working of this law most clearly is *The Benefit of the Doubt.* In reading it one feels that a few words of explanation, of Christian charity and forgiveness, would clear up the whole trouble; but one also knows that within the code such explanations were not required and would not have been accepted if they were given. It's all very terrible. People jeer at Pinero and at the artifice of his plays but for me it is not the characters he depicts that are tragic, but the world in which these characters exist.

Shortly before Pinero wrote *The Profligate* the plays of Ibsen began to be known in England and it is probable that they influenced Pinero quite considerably. Ibsen was a poet, as well as a magnificent dramatic craftsman. And a man who blazed inwardly at social injustice. Although he was as conscious as Pinero of a social code, he thrust deep below it to the very heart of his characters. Pinero does not thrust deep. He only partially animates his characters. He recognizes injustice but he gives no impression of resenting it. He does not mock the code like Shaw, or analyse it like Galsworthy, or probe it like Ibsen. He accepts. If he reads of a tragic scandal in the paper, he tut-tuts, shakes his head, folds up *The Times* and goes for a whacking good dinner at the club. Then perhaps writes a play about it.

If you want to understand exactly what I mean, read Ibsen's *A Doll's House* and then Pinero's *Iris,* and then, to take two plays on a different subject, *Hedda Gabler* and *The Notorious Mrs Ebbsmith.* I think you'll see the difference.

Pinero was fortunate in being extremely well served by his players, though it is also fair to add that he served them extremely well. The fact of the matter was that he took the trouble to become an absolute master of the theatre of his time. He understood the theatre itself, its scope and limitations, what he could do and couldn't do, he understood the leading actors and actresses, likewise knowing their strength and limitations, and supplied them with some of their finest parts. The performance of Stella Patrick Campbell in *The Second Mrs Tanqueray* increased the reputation of dramatist and actress beyond any chance of apportioning the credit. And he understood his audiences just as he understood the society he was depicting. Between Arthur Pinero, the actor-managers who staged his plays, and the Edwardian middle classes which supported them, there was all that identity of interest which had been missing from the English theatre for nearly three hundred years.

But is this identity of interest so important a thing? Wasn't there something missing from the theatre of Pinero? that something which is missing from the work of every man who is so completely a middle-of-the-roader? If I must put a name to this missing something, I would call it vision.

He was too much of an autocrat to have vision. Hesketh Pearson has given a grimly amusing picture of this terrifyingly impressive man of whom even the greatest actors were in holy terror. 'He had a loud deep voice', says Hesketh Pearson, 'and a severe expression. He rarely removed his hat from his head or his gloves from his hands. He treated his cast like automatons, instructing them minutely about their movements, their gestures, their vocal modulations, their facial expressions. If an actor was told to scratch his chin, he had to scratch his chin. And every word had to be heard clearly at the back of the gallery.'

But he was a first-rate story-teller.

SOME BOOKS FOR FURTHER READING:

A full-length biography of Pinero has yet to be written; but he is the subject of a large number of monographs, essays, and references in books on the Modern British theatre.

Likewise there is no recent complete edition of his plays. All of them were first published by William Heinemann, who was his personal friend as he was of many theatrical celebrities in the early years of the century; and they are not difficult to obtain from public libraries.

There are a very large number of books covering the theatre of the last hundred years; none are of outstanding excellence and many are tiresomely chatty. I am inclined to recommend Lynton Hudson's *The English Stage 1850—1950*, which is short but full of interesting and unusual quotations, and Ernest Reynolds's *Modern English Drama*, which contains all the necessary parts clearly arranged. George Rowell's *The Victorian Theatre* is very scholarly and reliable.

CHAPTER TEN

Bernard Shaw

BERNARD SHAW[1] IS as different from Sir Arthur Pinero as *Man and Superman* is different from *Iris* which appeared only two years earlier. This is not just a technical distinction between two dramatists with different personal styles, as that between Congreve and Vanburgh, for example, but a profoundly different attitude to drama, to people, and to life itself. Whatever may happen to the reputation of Bernard Shaw in the future, no historians of the theatre will be able to deny the revolutionary changes he brought to the British theatre in the first twenty years of the present century. And no one has described these changes more clearly than he has himself in the Prefaces of which I shall have more to say below.

Pinero was a conservative. He may have voted liberal for all I know or care, but his attitude to life was that of a man who would preserve the existing society. Bernard Shaw was disgusted with capitalist society and did everything that a writer, a dramatist, a public speaker, and a general agitator of people's opinions could do to change it. He was not an armchair socialist. In 1884 he helped to found the Fabian Society and remained on the executive

---

[1] Mr Shaw stated to his biographer, Hesketh Pearson, that he disliked any use of the word 'George'.

until 1911, twenty-seven years. He also helped to found the left-wing weekly, the *New Statesman.*

For a number of years, and at a time when his reputation as one of the most original playwrights of the day was growing, he was an active member of the St Pancras Borough Council, serving on a large number of sub-committees with enormous zeal.

Pinero was a staid, respectable and highly respected dramatist. Shaw was a professional comedian who enraged hundreds, perplexed thousands, and delighted millions by refusing to be pompous even about the most solemn subjects and those on which he entertained the strongest feelings. He was eccentric in his dress and striking in his personal appearance. Most photographs show him wearing a knicker-bocker suit of drain-pipe cut, and a curious collection of hats. He was tall and thin with a narrow white face, a strong nose, and an untrimmed ginger-coloured beard which went white along with his hair in his fifties.

Pinero did, wrote, and said little that was remarkable outside his work for the theatre. Shaw made half a dozen reputations besides that of dramatist. From 1884 till 1894 he wrote admirable music criticisms for various London papers after having served an apprenticeship in journalism as a book-reviewer and an art critic. Between 1895 and 1898, as dramatic critic of the *Saturday Review,* he wrote the finest collection of dramatic criticisms in the language. He was also, as I have said, a socialist economist. His famous book, *The Intelligent Woman's Guide to Socialism,* is one of the most brilliant political expositions in the language. (He addressed the book to women to ensure that he would preserve a fresh and lively style. It was

XIX
As You Like It
in the eighteen
-fifties

XX
Sir George
Alexander
(centre)

an unnecessary precaution.) He was a public speaker
of uncommon excellence, with a rich Irish accent, a
highly effective platform manner, and a devastatingly
ready wit. He left a large number of the wisest and
wittiest letters of which the most famous are those he
addressed to the actress Ellen Terry over a number of
years and which form an entertaining commentary on the
theatre of the nineties. He wrote discerning essays on Ibsen
and Wagner. And most famous of all perhaps, are the
Prefaces with which he adorned the published editions
of his plays, wherein he discusses a prodigious range of
subjects with incomparable wit, understanding, and depth
of feeling—and all, let it be emphasized, in peerless prose.

In a review of the printed edition of *The Second Mrs
Tanqueray* Shaw wrote:

Mr Pinero, then, is no interpreter of character, but simply
an adroit describer of people as the ordinary man sees them
and judges them. Add to this a clear head, a love of the
stage, and a fair talent for fiction, all highly cultivated by
hard and honourable work as a writer of effective stage plays
for the modern commercial theatre; and you have him on his
real level.

Though Pinero hasn't left so terse an estimation of
Shaw we know that he admired the man and detested his
plays; yet nothing, I think, hits off Shaw's generosity, one
of the most glowing aspects of his character, so surely as
his having persuaded the Prime Minister, Lord Asquith,
to give the elderly dramatist a knighthood.

Hesketh Pearson says that no manager dared to decline
the honour of presenting one of Pinero's plays. Shaw
had the greatest difficulty for many years in persuading
10

any manager at all to stage even one of his plays for a single performance. Pinero obeyed every rule. Shaw broke the lot. But I will return to the subject of his plays.

Some of the most entertaining Prefaces are the autobiographical ones which give us a splendid picture of Shaw himself. It was continually said of Shaw by those that he ruffled or exasperated that he was an exhibitionist. It is clear that he rarely hid his light under a bushel, and that he was at pains not to leave the general public in any doubt about the sort of man he was, and the precise nature of his views on every conceivable subject. But the one thing that emerges from the many people who knew him is his enormous goodness, his sympathy to people genuinely in trouble, his generosity, his kindliness. It was impossible to quarrel with Shaw. People fumed at him, said the most cruel things about him: he passed it all off with a smile and a jest.

But Shaw is not the only source for our knowledge of Shaw. Leading a distinguished and active public life for over sixty years, he had many friends and they have not been reluctant to describe him. Nor can a man write about biological evolution, the capitalist system, Christianity, marriage and divorce, monarchy, and goodness knows how many other subjects in a most trenchant and provocative style without producing a large number of critical books criticizing and discussing every aspect of his criticisms. The number of books on Shaw in no way approaches the number written about Shakespeare because Shaw has ensured that every aspect of his life and work has been fully revealed; whereas Shakespeare is all mystery. But there are plenty.

Both Shaw himself and his excellent biographers have

dealt with details of his life so fully and so wittily, in books that are readily available in every library, that I am going to content myself with a few comments on his work to encourage my readers to find out more themselves.

Music was one of the passions of Shaw's life. His mother, with whom he lived for many years in London, after having left Dublin, was a music-teacher and Shaw has described how he knew the leading arias from the great operas almost as soon as he knew the great stories of English literature. I emphasize this in view of a persistent and rather ill-founded criticism that is continually made of Shaw, namely that he is all intellect and lacks emotion. For he must be an extremely insensitive person who does not respond to the quality of Shaw's prose, and the shapeliness of some of the great speeches which are sustained and melodic like an operatic aria. Shaw's dialogue, like all dramatic dialogue, is written to be spoken. Anyone who does not understand what I mean, should read aloud some of his great speeches and try to respond to the wealth of emotion that underlies them.

And now for his plays. The first thing that strikes one about them is the immense scope of their subject-matter. Shaw wrote fifty-three plays. This in itself is a considerable achievement. Let me give some examples from the list of titles in his Collected Plays: *Widower's Houses* (landlords and slum property); *Mrs Warren's Profession* (prostitution); *Arms and the Man* (a delightful satire on militarism); *The Man of Destiny* (Napoleon); *The Devil's Disciple* (a story of the American War of Independence); *Caesar and Cleopatra* (read this together with *Antony and Cleopatra* and *All for Love*); *Man and Superman* (biological evolution); *John Bull's Other*

Island (Ireland); *Major Barbara* (poverty, capitalism, and the Salvation Army); *The Doctor's Dilemma* (doctors); *Getting Married* (marriage); *The Dark Lady of the Sonnets* (Shakespeare); *Androcles and the Lion* (Christianity); *Pygmalion* (environment); *Back to Methuselah* (a continuation of the theme of *Man and Superman,* a play in five parts extending from the Garden of Eden to the remote future); *Saint Joan* (thought by some to be his masterpiece, though many people, like Shaw himself, plump for *Heartbreak House*); *The Apple Cart* (a splendid play on the monarchy), and so on. In this book I have discussed the work of some dozen other dramatists, the best to have written in English (excluding the Americans): is there one to touch such a range?— excepting always Shakespeare.

Shaw is now a part of our heritage. We are in danger of taking him for granted. But I can remember vividly the thrill of first coming into contact with his plays. It was a hot summer afternoon in 1926 and a freckled, sandy-haired maths master evidently shared our loathing at the prospect of quadratic equations, for he told us about *Back to Methuselah,* that stupendous sequence of plays which like a medieval cycle takes three nights to perform. Suddenly we became conscious of there being a dramatist in our midst who was turning the world of thought upside down. He'd put the whole story of the evolution of man into a single play. He'd set a play, or a part of a play, in Hell. We argued fiercely for the single library copy of *Man and Superman* so excitedly adorned with *The Revolutionist's Handbook.* That was thirty years ago, and I have rarely picked up a copy of a play by Shaw without responding to its tremendous intellectual vitality, and to Shaw's astonishing ability to make us see familiar subjects in an entirely new light. How rare and original we think; but Shaw himself describes somewhere that his apparent originality is simply due to his ability to see things clearly and simply : he is gifted with normal vision : he sees things differently from most other people and sees them better.

Of Shaw as a craftsman it is difficult to write. If one should set his plays against the yard-stick of the 'well-made play' and give Pinero credit marks or even a distinction, Shaw would be lucky to score ten out of a hundred. But then his plays, for the most part, hold the stage, and I doubt whether there is any other measure worth bothering about. *Getting Married* and *Misalliance* have neither act nor scene divisions. They have perfect unity of everything. They start, they proceed, they stop. But neither have they a story. This is splendid ammunition for the pedants who can say without fear of contradiction 'But these just aren't plays'. Ask such people what they mean by a play and you will find their answers will be very pretentious or very conventional. So we can do worse than say that a play is simply a dramatic action which holds the attention of the audience. If it does this and is still unsatisfactory, well then is the time to look deeper. Shaw wrote bad plays just as Shakespeare did. The world would not be greatly the poorer for the loss of *The Comedy of Errors* and *On the Rocks*. But to attempt to dismiss Shaw as a dramatist is simply to dismiss oneself.

The real difficulty in coping with Shaw's craftsmanship seems to me to lie in a play like *Androcles and the Lion* which some people consider to be among his finest achievements. The theme of the play is the persecution of a minority by a dictatorship; its story that of Christians being thrown to the lions. Goodness knows, it's a serious enough theme. But Shaw gives the producer an extremely difficult task by presenting a series of tragic situations yet treating them in the manner of farce. Difficulties of this kind abound throughout his plays; but I think that we must beware of imagining them to be errors of craftsmanship when they are very deliberate examples of Shaw's method and technique. Again, we may not like them, but we just cannot dismiss them as incompetence.

Some people may feel that I am going too far in my refusal to accept a standard of dramatic craftsmanship. The answer is that I would be delighted to accept a standard if I knew which standard to accept: Shaw's great achievement was to destroy a standard that had become a straight-jacket. We are now in a period of transition: new standards will emerge all in good time but only if in the meantime we judge work on its own merits and not by applying standards that have become meaningless.

Another criticism of Shaw is that he writes from the head and not from the heart. To this I have several answers. First of all I would ask anyone who feels like making this criticism whether he or she has seen *Candida*, *The Doctor's Dilemma*, *Saint Joan* and *Androcles and the Lion*, decently performed. If anyone can see these plays without being deeply moved, anyway at certain passages, he's a tougher theatre-goer than I am ever likely to be, and so far as *Candida* and *Saint Joan* go, I would not limit myself to 'certain passages'. They're masterpieces.

My second answer is this: why not? Is the theatre to be a place where people abandon intelligence? Frankly I do not think that we properly understand this distinction between the head and the heart. In fact I believe that to separate the two is to be physiologically thoroughly unsound. The heart, after all, is only a metaphor for sensations that are different from those of thought : in fact the whole mechanism of thought and feeling takes place in the cells of the brain. I think that we are inclined to resent being made to think in the theatre simply because we have grown used to becoming lulled into a condition of thoughtless emotion. For this reason pretty girls and fine scenery are to be distrusted. Even with Shakespeare we are inclined to let the great words flood over us without worrying overmuch whether we understand their meaning or not. But Shaw, who wrote for an audience that was used to wallowing in the emotions of the alluring Mrs Patrick Campbell, would not let the audience go to sleep, or doze through endless sensualities : he prodded them with every other sentence, and we don't like being prodded, least of all when we're not expecting it.

Of course there are criticisms to be made of Shaw. Sometimes he seems to be speaking himself throughout a scene, simply carving up the lines between the different characters. His buffoonery can be exasperating and is sometimes in very bad taste.

As you become familiar with Shaw's plays you will level at him every criticism under the sun : you will find him perverse, tendentious, a clown, a preacher, an orator; you will be moved, excited, exasperated. But I hope you will always put down the book, or leave the theatre, richer for having made contact with so tremendous a personality.

When I was a boy I used to paper the walls of my room with my favourite passages from literature. If my readers can stand so horrifying a revelation I will end by quoting the first passage I took from Shaw, lines which I confess still give me that kind of elation I derive from the last speech of Shelley's *Prometheus*. They are the concluding lines of the fifth and last part of *Back to Methuselah*. They are spoken by Lilith, a lady who in some traditions is thought to have been the first wife of Adam. The lines are a kind of apostrophe to the creative power of the intellect which is the theme of the play, and a splendid piece of rhetoric.

I am Lilith : I brought life into the whirlpool of force, and compelled my enemy, Matter, to obey a living soul. But in enslaving Life's enemy I made him Life's master; for that is the end of all slavery; and now I shall see the slave set free and the enemy reconciled, the whirlpool become all life and no matter. And because these infants that call themselves Ancients are reaching out towards that, I will have patience with them still; though I know well that when they attain it they shall become one with me and supersede me, and Lilith will be only a legend and a lay that has lost its meaning. Of Life only there is no end; and though of its million starry mansions many are empty and many still unbuilt, and though its vast domain is as yet unbearably desert, my seed shall one day fill it and master its matter to its uttermost confines. And for what may be beyond, the eyesight of Lilith is too short. It is enough that there is a beyond.

Bernard Shaw, who was born in 1856, died in 1950 at the age of ninety-four. It was a splendid life.

SOME BOOKS FOR FURTHER READING:

Hesketh Pearson's *Bernard Shaw* is exemplary. It is
continued in *G.B.S.: a Postscript* (since the former was
written ten years before Shaw's death). Frank Harris's
Bernard Shaw is chatty, perverse, and very personal but most
entertaining, while A. C. Ward's *Bernard Shaw* is a clear
simple survey of his life and works, and St. John Ervine's
Bernard Shaw is a splendid, great biography.

Commentaries include G. K. Chesterton's *George Bernard
Shaw*, critical but full of splendid material; Eric Bentley's
Bernard Shaw, a lively commentary on the plays and philo-
sophy; and C. E. M. Joad's *Shaw* is a personal discussion of
what Shaw meant to a philosopher who knew and admired
him deeply.

G.B.S. 90 is a collection of essays on every aspect of Shaw's
genius presented to him on his ninetieth birthday. Has ever
a man received such a moving and generous tribute?

And there are many more; but however entertaining they
may be, do not read them at the expense of Shaw's own
inimitable writings.

CHAPTER ELEVEN

Sean O'Casey

I HAVEN'T THE LEAST idea what conditions a dramatist has to fulfil to be considered British and I don't intend to ask. I have included Sean O'Casey in this book because he is a friend of mine, because I think that he has received far less than his due from writers on the twentieth century theatre and because I happen to think that he is a master of the drama. As a matter of fact there is another reason, which is that the Irish have made a considerable contribution to the drama of the British Isles and this gives me a chance to tell you something about it.

First of all a word about the Irish. We all know them to be an imaginative people with a fine gift of language. This is because they're descended from the Kelts, a war-like people but possessed of a feeling for poetry and myth, who swept across Europe in the centuries immediately preceding the time of Christ, settled in Britain and were driven further westward by subsequent invaders. Some of the Kelts took refuge in the mountains of Scotland and Wales and others crossed the sea to Ireland. Those who stayed this side of the Irish Sea carried on a persistent underground warfare against more obstinate invaders such as the Romans with such success that British farmers began to tell fairy stories of a mysterious people who came out at night, committed all kinds of mischievous pranks of a rather hurtful kind, and defied extermination.

The Kelts who crossed to Ireland were followed by Danes and Normans but they were neither driven out nor underground. Consequently the religion of the Kelts, and in particular their mythology, which is the story part of religion, survived in the form of a rich treasury of folk-lore which the Irish passed from generation to generation by word of mouth for many hundreds of years. When Christianity became established in Ireland, Irish Christians showed themselves to be among the most intelligent and artistic in Europe and went forth into many lands, founding monasteries and preaching the word of God. I mention this because one of the most successful Irishisms of this highly intelligent people has been to make themselves out the sort of improvident stupid peasants that Englishmen tell funny stories about in pubs. It is just as sinful and stupid to judge the Irish by the labourers who come to England for work as it is to judge the English by the behaviour of our aristocracy at Ascot.

It is disastrous that lack of understanding and of toleration between the two countries should ever have led to bloodshed; it is disastrous that tensions within Ireland herself should have led to the censorship of literature and the banning of certain books by her leading writers. But these things happen, and it is for men of goodwill to recognize the enrichment which this gay, passionate and intelligent people, divided from us by only thirty miles of blue sea, have made to our culture.

At the end of this chapter I shall give the names of one or two books where those who are interested in this subject of the Irish temperament can find out more about it; but the quality of the Irish which has impressed the English most strongly has been, as I say, the gift of language. You will find this gift at its richest in the plays of Synge whose work has a particular interest because he claims that he has done little more than reproduce the natural language of the peasants living in the remoter parts of Ireland. In his Preface to *The Playboy of the Western World* Synge writes:

In countries where the imagination of the people and the language they use is rich and living, it is possible for a writer to be rich and copious in his words and at the same time to give the reality, which is the root of all poetry, in a natural form.

But the richly poetic language which one finds in the plays of Synge and O'Casey is one thing and the polished epigrammatic language that is a feature of the plays of Congreve, Sheridan and Shaw is something different. I think that we should distrust people who talk about 'splendour of language' as if it was a gift of stringing fine words together without regard for their meaning or the thought behind them. Congreve and Sheridan did not have profound minds, but each had an acute intelligence; and Shaw had both. We must therefore guard against inclination to fancy the Irish writer a mere blatherer whose words pour out in a torrent of metaphor signifying precious little and remember that language to be really fine must be the expression of thought refined, polished and expanded so as to convey exactly the meaning and the emotions of the writer. Words for the sake of words is humbug.

In case anyone should think that this gift has anything to do with education I must point out that two of the greatest Irish masters of language had no education at all to speak of. Shaw was brought up in a household where he had every opportunity to read and little encouragement to go to school and O'Casey was brought up in the slums of Dublin with almost no education or even books of any kind; he sold newspapers while still a boy, became a general labourer as a young man, had nothing published until he was thirty and didn't write a play until he was nearly forty.

Fortunately for her son, O'Casey's mother timed his birth with great accuracy. Sean became literate towards the turn of the century at the time of the movement known as the Irish Literary Renaissance. He learnt to read and opened his eyes to the world and his ears to literature when W. B. Yeats and other writers were creating a splendid period of Irish literature. Yeats in particular, a poet whom many believe to be the finest of this century, set an example in using the ancient Keltic myths as source material for literature and drama.

Yeats was also part-founder of the Abbey Theatre in Dublin, the double glory of which was its dramatists which included Yeats himself, Lady Gregory, John Millington Synge, Lennox Robinson and Sean O'Casey, and its players who formed a company that became celebrated throughout the English-speaking world. I hope that the Irish plays of this period will never be entirely divorced from the names of Arthur Sinclair, Barry Fitzgerald, Sarah Allgood and Maire O'Neill.

The disaster of modern Ireland has been the unhappy treatment of the country by the English, our hand in the bloody events of Easter 1916 and the fierce civil war of 1922, and our attitude to the formation of a Republic. It is a miserable and shameful memory that Ireland should have won her independence in an atmosphere poisoned with bloodshed, tyranny, treachery and the horrifying spectacle of Irishman against Irishman. The Irish had been extremely touchy on the subject of their national pride before the times of the troubles and as early as 1907 a Dublin audience had expressed its fury at what it took to be a jibe at the Irish peasants on the first production of Synge's masterpiece *The Playboy of the Western World*.

Sean O'Casey, being a Socialist, was deeply involved in the events of 1916. On one occasion he came near to being stood against a wall and shot. All this period of his life, together with his horror at the way in which the events of 1922 were mishandled, form the subject of the third and most moving volume of his autobiography, *Inishfallen, Fare Thee Well*.

It is not true, as has been stated, that long before the production of his first play in 1922 O'Casey had been a regular visitor at the Abbey : he could never have afforded it. Nor was he a literary dilettante looking round for an outlet for his talent. O'Casey started to write plays because he had an impulse to do so. I would say that he was a more naturally born dramatist than anyone I have written about in this book with the exceptions of Marlowe and Shakespeare. Apart from his plays O'Casey has written little but a few buzzing critical essays and the six tremendous volumes of his autobiography, the most dramatic thing of their kind and none the worse for that. O'Casey has three of the prime and most necessary qualities for a dramatist: a deep intuitive love for and understanding of human beings; a magnificent command of language; and an artist's vision of his experiences. By this last phrase I mean the ability to conceive thoughts and feelings in terms of human characters, and to reveal those characters in what they do and say.

For one of the inescapable problems of a dramatist is to find a way of making explicit characters who in their very nature are inexplicit.

His first three plays were *The Shadow of a Gunman* (1922), *Juno and the Paycock* (1924), and *The Plough and the Stars* (1926). In each of these plays he deals with episodes from the events of 1916 and 1922. But he was in trouble from the start. Instead of flying the romantic green and yellow of Irish independence, he had drawn convincing human beings, sorrowing mothers, drunken human husbands, the sort of people that had lived in Dublin and taken part or become involved in the events of those tragic years, and not the noble chauvinistic caricatures of Irish leaders which his critics clearly wanted.

The management of the Abbey was in perplexity. His plays were successful even when they were criticized and their quality was beyond question. I think that there must have been a tinge of relief when the experimental nature of his fourth major play gave them an opportunity to refuse production. The subject of *The Silver Tassie* ostensibly was the first World War. Its real subject was War—anywhere, any time. The first act has a bitter satirical quality; then O'Casey's feelings seem to explode into a second act set just behind the front line in which he uses a technique that had hitherto been foreign to the Irish theatre. By making the soldiers speak in a kind of chant, using a poetic diction, he essays to give an impression of what cannot be conveyed realistically, the horror of modern warfare.

When in 1929 the play was staged in London the critics generally accepted the experiment as a success. But after the play had been refused by the Directors of the Abbey Theatre, W. B. Yeats wrote to O'Casey questioning the sincerity of his interest in the First World War! This brought to a head a discomfiture that had been growing upon O'Casey for some years and like a number of Irishmen before him, he took the irrevocable step and came to England.

Life was not easy for him in England. *The Silver Tassie* brought him in little money after its original production for it is too difficult a play to be often staged. As to his earlier successes, one group of offended people after another were continually trying to suppress them and all too frequently succeeding. (How human beings love to suppress what they do not agree with!) But two elements have blazed within him and been the constant inspiration of his creative work. One has been Ireland and the other has been his humanity. Of the two his humanity, his passionate love of life and of human nature, has been the greater inspiration, but this main theme of his creative work has continually been coloured by his profound and rich store of Keltic culture.

It was his humanity which blazed out in his next play, produced in 1934, at the Royalty Theatre, London, one of the many now destroyed. It was called *Within the Gates,* and it was set in a London park, or can I say, an artist's vision of a London park. O'Casey's deep compassion for the labouring poor and his hatred of hypocrisy, kill-joys,

XXI   Sir Arthur Pinero

XXII Granville Barker in
      Man and Superman

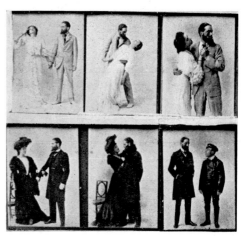

XXIII
Bernard Shaw
at a public
meeting

SEAN O'CASEY   161

bureaucrats and the deadening hand of an insensitive
authority, showed itself very clearly.

An episode took place during the run of this play that
impressed itself upon me very strongly. For personal
reasons you might be able to guess I saw this play four
times. On one of these occasions I sat beside a distinguished, or at least a very successful, popular playwright.
'What is the matter with O'Casey?' he kept saying in the
intervals; 'He's got a beautiful wife and a healthy family :
where's the need for all this bitterness?' I sensed the
stupidity of the remark but in those days I did not
understand that there need be no relationship between a
man's private life and his artistic vision. Is one to suppose
that if Jesus Christ had married happily he would
have lost his burning compassion for the poor and
his hatred for the Pharisees? Thanks to his lovely wife,
O'Casey did succeed in overcoming his poverty and
creating a home, at first in London and then in Devonshire
where he could bring up his children and find the necessary
concentration for his writing. But far from blunting his
vision, dulling his compassion, and allaying his anger, his
own domestic comfort sharpened these things and gave the
plays that followed a fury and an intensity that many
people appear to be unable to stomach.

You may read the plays of O'Casey and his autobiography and feel that here is an angry man. In one place
he tells the story of a visit to lunch with Bernard Shaw
and how Charlotte Shaw proceeded to rap his knuckles
severely for the apparent alacrity with which he picked
quarrels. There are two things to be said to this. The first
is that he's had to put up with enough to make him angry.
The second is quite simply that while he is perhaps the

11

most un-angry man I have ever met he is the least willing to suffer fools, hypocrites, humbugs, impostors and quacks and all the other enemies of a free and happy life, with the least sign of grace. When you are in the presence of O'Casey, far from feeling yourself to be in the presence of a dragon, you are with a gentle, expansive, and intensely human man who presses you to God knows how many cups of tea and then takes you round to the local for a beer. I can assure you from my own experience that he is both lovable and extremely generous.

In 1940 an amateur production of his next play, *The Star Turns Red*, was given in London. An extremely successful run was cut short after two months by the German advance to the west.

This play is far and away the most powerful dramatization I have come across of the struggle of the nineteen-thirties between Fascism and Communism. But O'Casey, basing his material on the shape of the Civil War that had taken place in Spain, where the coming World War was fought in miniature, shows the Church aligning itself with the Fascists, assuming political leadership as he had seen happen in Ireland. Many people found this difficult enough to swallow. And then he committed the unforgivable sin of showing sympathy for the Communists!

The play received warm appreciation from the press. The then celebrated critic James Agate of the *Sunday Times,* whom no one could accuse of having been a Socialist, devoted two columns to appraising the play under the heading A MASTERPIECE.

The next plays were *Purple Dust* (extraordinarily powerful), *Red Roses for Me,* and *Oak Leaves and Lavender* in which O'Casey makes a rather moving commentary upon the Second World War. It's in these plays that the Kelt in O'Casey, so long suppressed, begins to erupt. His themes continue to be universal. They apply to Man irrespective of nationality. But he gives his plays an Irish setting, he sees humanity through the eyes of the Irish and although this enriches their texture it seems to make O'Casey unduly scornful of his countrymen. Ireland, as it were, comes in for all the disgust and fury he feels for mankind in general and the gulf that separates Ireland from her greatest playwright has deepened.

The third act of *Red Roses for Me* gives a memorable example of O'Casey's later style. It is set in Dublin, in front of a bridge over the River Liffey. The distant houses are tall and gaunt and the sky is grey. A crowd of people with dulled expressionless faces are leaning against the parapet of the bridge or lounging in front of the gaunt houses. Among the crowd are three lovely girls, dressed as drably as the rest. They are discussing in a timeless kind of way—Ireland; all that they love and hate about their country, and all the old myths and legends that are so much a part of the Irish character come welling up into the conversation.

Then follows a remarkable vision. The sun sets and the scene becomes dark; but suddenly the setting sun catches the houses on the far side of the river and decks them in mauve and burnished bronze; and the men, who have been lounging against them now stand stalwartly erect, looking like fine bronze statues slashed with scarlet; the faces of the girls are aglow and the head of the young hero is caught in a streak of sunlight and looking like a young hero of Keltic myth he seems to speak out of the darkness :

There's th' great dome o' th' Four Courts lookin' like a golden rose in a great bronze bowl! An' th' river flowin' below it, a purple flood, marbled with ripples o' scarlet; watch th' seagulls glidin' over it—like restless white pearls astir on a royal breast. Our city's in th' grip o' God!

O'Casey's most recent plays are *Cock-a-Doodle Dandy* and *The Bishop's Bonfire.* This last was produced in 1955 at the Gaiety Theatre, Dublin, and produced the usual uproar. *Cock-a-Doodle Dandy* seems to me an incomparably vivid and powerful play, a really tremendous hymn to the joy of life and the perdition of its enemies. That such a play has not been given a sumptuous production in London using the very finest actors the English and Irish stage can offer is an appalling commentary on countries that can produce a master playwright and turn in terror from his plays because he tells unpalatable truths. The grizly fact is that London has not seen a decent production of an O'Casey play since *The Silver Tassie* in 1929. *Within the Gates* and *Oak Leaves and Lavender* received pitiably poor productions. The Dublin production of *Red Roses for Me* which came to the Embassy Theatre was a little better; *Purple Dust* collapsed on tour.

Well, I suppose it's understandable that some people should react so strongly against the subject of his plays that they should be unable to see any good in them at all; but I find it astonishing that they should resent his experimental technique. What would these same critics be yammering if O'Casey had continued to write plays throughout his life in the manner he perfected in *Juno and the Paycock* and *The Plough and the Stars,* even supposing he had been able to do so? I'm afraid it's only the hacks and the industrialists, the merchants who would get-rich-quick-at-any-price who work away at a prosperous seam until it's exhausted. Moreover there's a kind of assumption that the poetic style O'Casey has developed in his later plays is less properly artistic than his naturalistic methods. Let's have a look at this.

Here is a celebrated passage from *Juno and the Paycock*. The context is hardly necessary. It's near the beginning of the play and Captain Jack Boyle, a good-for-nothing husband who is the 'paycock' of the title, is gossiping to his friend Joxer when he should be working.

Voice of coal vendor: Blocks . . . coal blocks! Blocks! . . . coal blocks!

Joxer: God be with the young days when you were steppin' the deck of a manly ship, with the win' blowin' a hurricane through the masts, an' the only sound you'd hear was, 'Port you helm!' an' the only answer, 'Port it is, sir!'

Boyle: Them was days, Joxer, them was days. Nothin' was too hot or too heavy for me then. Sailin' from the Gulf o' Mexico to the Antanartic Ocean. I seen things, I seen things, Joxer, that no mortal man should speak about that knows his Catechism. Ofen an' ofen, when I was fixed to the wheel with a marlin-spike, an' the win's blowin' fierce an' the waves lashin' an' lashin', till you'd think every minute was goin' to be your last, an' it blowed an' blowed—blew is the right word, Joxer, but blowed is what the sailors use . . .

Joxer: Aw, it's a darlin' word, a daarlin' word.

Boyle: An', as it blowed an' blowed, I ofen looked up at the sky an' assed meself the question—what is the stars, what is the stars?

Coal-vendor: Any blocks, coal-blocks, any blocks, coal-blocks!

Joxer: Ah, that's the question, that's the question—what is the stars?

Boyle: An' then, I'd have another look, an' I'd ass meself—what is the moon?

Joxer: Ah, that's the question—what is the moon, what is the moon?

I suppose it's understandable that people should find that kind of dialogue so splendid as to grudge O'Casey having written in any other kind of way.

But this kind of writing imposes enormous limitations on the dramatist because he can only dramatize scenes which might conceivably have happened in real life and he can only make the characters use language which they might themselves have spoken. Of course even the most naturalistic plays are in fact extremely unnatural. This is obvious. In a performance of *Juno* you would realize the extremely clever way in which the coal vendor has been used to give an impression of the continuing life of the tenements and to break up Joxer's repetition of Boyle's ridiculous questions. Consequently dramatists have been continually searching for other styles of writing which would give them more scope for their imagination, as Dryden hoped of the 'heroic' play, and a chance to use a different kind of subject-matter.

I don't think O'Casey would care for it to be said that he was writing in the manner of Shakespeare but that is how he uses language. It is almost as if he were expecting his plays to be performed on a bare stage and so gives his dialogue sufficient texture not merely to take the audience to the heart of the characters, for that is what the critics of his new style claim that he has failed to do, but to give an imaginative picture of the world in which the characters are living, not by describing the scenery, but by continuously working into the dialogue the kind of metaphors and images that will set the imagination of the audience creating the world of the play; just as Shakespeare did in *Twelfth Night* for example. O'Casey uses language to help him extend his subject matter.

As a matter of fact it's O'Casey's stage directions that give one the strongest indication of the manner in which he conceives his plays. I know of no stage-directions which are so conscious of colour. It is not that he constantly gives the colour of the clothes, the scenery, and so on, in his directions: plenty of dramatists have done that; but that colour for O'Casey is a very strong element in the manner in which he conceives his plays. When he says that a character is to wear purple or scarlet or saffron yellow or black he is not indulging a fancy but giving a very clear indication of how he has envisaged the play. He has used colour as other dramatists have used music or verse or masks or a special kind of scenery to help create the necessary effect. You just cannot use colour as O'Casey has used it in his later plays, in a naturalistic play.

If you get a chance of reading *The Silver Tassie* ask yourself how O'Casey could successfully have expressed what he wanted to say in his second act by simply writing naturalistic dialogue typical of a group of soldiers in a dug-out. An exact transliteration of front-line language would be wholly inadequate in the theatre.

Let me give you one or two examples of his language from *The Star Turns Red*. Here is a speech by a girl which gives a vivid picture of the revolutionary state of the town in which the play takes place.

There'll be a red core in the night before it closes. The Red Priest of the politicians is patrolling the streets, cursing with book and bell and candle any who have cried or murmured a welcome to Communism; and he's dragging the Brown Priest of the poor at his heels, afraid to let him out of his sight, the way he'll be kept from mixing or sympathising with the people; while, with a silent march, dotted with drum-beats, the Saffron Shirts are shooing the people into a wary stillness.

Here is the Red Priest of the Politicians thundering against Communism:

Communism would banish God from your altars: it would change your holy churches into places where bats hang by day and owls hoot by night; it would soil the sacrament of marriage by lust; it would hack in sunder the holy union of the family; street gutters would run with the blood of your pastors; and all holy thoughts and deeds would sink down into a weary heap of blackened ashes!

And this brings us to the very crux of dramatic art as exemplified in the plays of O'Casey: artistic perception, intellectual passion, fine language, and clearly conceived characters.

But properly to understand the measure of O'Casey's achievement you should read *Cock-a-Doodle Dandy* which is really a moral play, only instead of being about Death, like *Everyman,* it's about Life. I do not know of a dramatist who has sung to life more eagerly than O'Casey, unless it be Marlowe, or Shakespeare, or Congreve, or Bernard Shaw. Might not that be the sign then of a master dramatist—that he sings to life even when he brings us face to face with Death?

SOME BOOKS FOR FURTHER READING:

I know of no books about O'Casey but here are the titles of the six volumes of his autobiography:

> *I Knock at the Door*
> *Pictures in the Hallway*
> *Drums Under the Window*
> *Inishfallen, Fare Thee Well:*
> *Rose and Crown*
> *Sunset and Evening Star*

His plays are all published separately as well as in a Collected Edition of four volumes.

Some of his critical essays have been collected under the title of *The Green Crow.*

As for the character of the Kelts I recommend *The Irish* by that fine writer Sean O'Faolain.

CHAPTER TWELVE

A Temple of the Ascent of Man

THE DRAMATIC CRITICISMS which Bernard Shaw contributed to the *Saturday Review* were first published in a Collected Edition in 1906. Bernard Shaw wrote a short introduction to the book in which he describes how he took the theatre to be 'a factory of thought, a prompter of conscience, an elucidator of social conduct, an armoury against despair and dullness, and a temple of the Ascent of Man. . . . I preached about it,' he says, 'instead of merely chronicling its news and alternatively petting and snubbing it as a licentious but privileged form of public entertainment.'

The suggestion that the theatre should be taken seriously makes a good many hackles rise. 'We don't want to be preached at', is the usual reaction, 'we want to be amused, and entertained.' 'How comes it then that you are amused by being made to cry? How do you explain that you were entertained last week by a film that made you sob?' It is an unfair question because many great thinkers have asked the question and been unable to answer it. Naturally I cannot myself. But I can narrow the subject down a bit.

Let us start off for the sake of argument by agreeing that there are two forms of theatre, the industry of entertainment, or what the Americans call 'show business', and the art of the theatre.

I think there's not very much doubt about the spirit in which we go to the theatre to be entertained. We're tired, bored, or worried, and we want to be refreshed, cheered, or taken out of ourselves. In certain moods a show that has plenty of humour, good tunes, colourful scenery, or an exciting story will satisfy us. In other moods we want to drink more deeply. A detective story is like thin tasty soup. It doesn't nourish you for long, however satisfactory it may be at the moment. But to read Galsworthy or Dickens with the least attention is to meet a set of characters that stay in your mind. In the same way you're not likely to see a reasonably good production of *Hamlet* or *Volpone, Love for Love* or *Man and Superman,* or *Cock-a-Doodle Dandy* that won't stick in your mind for some considerable time. I don't even mean that you will be able to recall details of the performance for months ahead but that you will carry round with you the impressions of the performance, the memory of the experience you went through as if you had absorbed it into your system like a first-rate meal.

I should warn you of this however : that to get full enjoyment from a serious play—and by the word 'serious' I include a Pinero farce or Shaw's delightful comedy, *You Never Can Tell*—you have to start off by giving that small amount of extra attention which is not called for by the show that bellows in your ears and sits in your lap. But the refreshment at the end is accordingly the greater.

Now remember that I only separated entertainment from art 'for the sake of argument'. Misunderstandings arise when we argue on the assumption that they never meet or overlap. The industry of entertainment is frequently highly artistic and theatrical art is usually extremely entertaining. In the theatre today the distinction is really one of administration. The entertainment industry is 'show business'. Its first concern is not the finest artistic standard but the response of the public. So a play that is produced in London by one of the big commercial managements will almost always have a couple of stars in the leading parts even if lesser known actors should be more suitable, a certain slickness of presentation which I would describe as an emphasis on its appearance, its theatrical effectiveness, at the cost of its true meaning. This is not an invariable practice of the commercial theatre but you should constantly be on your guard against it. The argument of those who consider themselves artists against those who will not admit that they are industrialists is that the latter, the show-business people, are predatory in their behaviour, pulling all the theatres into combines, signing up the leading actors, and one way and another confining the artists to tiny theatres in Notting Hill Gate and sitting-rooms in Hampstead.

This unhappy distinction really applies to the theatre of the last hundred and fifty years, that is since the Industrial Revolution. In Shakespeare's day a delightful comedy might be given at the Globe Theatre while the cruellest fights between animals were taking place in the beargarden not a hundred yards away. Queen Elizabeth patronized both forms of entertainment and many of her citizens seem to have thought the one as immoral as the other.

The distinction has arisen because society has become increasingly complex; people have become divided into classes, with different tastes, different habits, and different occupations; and each class has cultivated its own culture. Do you remember what Synge said about language?

Scholars are now fairly certain that the Elizabethan theatres were supported by a very average cross-section of the public. Noblemen and students both visited the theatres and all the in-between kind of people as well. There was little distinction in price between the expensive and the cheaper seats—only a few pence. As a matter of fact a seat in the Globe was cheaper than a pint of ale and a great deal cheaper than an inexpensive book. Of course Elizabethans had different tastes just as we do today: There were *Times*-minded Elizabethans and *Mirror*-minded Elizabethans, but the differences in tastes were not related to differences in classes.

This made the basis of their culture very much stronger than it is today because a man could write a quite difficult poem reasonably sure that it would be understood, even if it wasn't particularly appreciated, by the butcher, the baker, the candlestick maker.

In the chapter on Dryden we saw that for various reasons the Restoration theatre lost this broad-based support and became almost exclusively identified with, and supported by, the middle and upper classes. The nearest thing to an Elizabethan *The Way of the World* would have been a comedy by John Lyly such as *Campaspe* and this was the nearest thing the Elizabethans got to a class theatre, for Lyly's comedies were not played in the public theatres, but almost wholly to the nobility and before the court. Conversely Shakespeare's plays with their robust and popular appeal, became increasingly less to the taste of Restoration and eigheenth-century audiences and were re-written, hacked about, given new happy endings, and so on.

The industrialization of Britain in the eighteenth century increased these tendencies. The middle and upper classes became richer and more powerful—why, they covered the country with magnificent houses in the middle of tremendous parks, and all honour to them for their excellent taste—but there was created an enormous industrial working class. To this class, whom some people are surprised to be told have very much the same appetites and emotions as the gentry, the regular theatres like Drury Lane and Covent Garden did not cater. The result was that enterprising men came along, the forerunners of the modern commercial managers, and began to supply entertainment to these large numbers of men and women who had been poorly educated, who had jobs of unspeakable drudgery, and who were reduced by the conditions in which they were obliged to live to a state little better than that of slaves. So-called popular entertainment consisted of music-halls, circuses, melodramatic plays, brass band concerts and all the fun of the fair. Popular entertainment however wasn't wholly poor. When the responsible people, managers, actors, clowns, musicians, singers and the rest drew, as they often did, upon some ancient tradition, they succeeded in preserving some tune, song, ballad, or style of acting from the days before the split in culture had taken place. The artist-chaps and the middle and upper classes have realized this and from time to time have gone theatrical slumming by visiting a music hall in a poor district or a circus in a village field; and they usually come away refreshed because in the middle of incompetence, sentimentality, and a great deal of poor material, there usually survives some element or other of the ancient cultural tradition.

In the twentieth century we have got as far as recognizing at long last that a man does not live by his wage-packet alone and what he can buy with it nor by every word that proceedeth from the B.B.C. but that he needs rich spiritual refreshment. It's lack of this refreshment that accounts for the excessive adulation of film-stars. This would not matter but for the alarming fact that to turn girls into goddesses means a surrender of judgment and this in turn leads to the even more alarming surrender of the whole personality.

Experiments have been made throughout the world during the last fifty years to restore the harmony of culture. I have been concerned in experiments myself. The first production of *The Star Turns Red* was part of an attempt to create a theatre which should find its audiences chiefly among trade-unionists. We failed; but nothing has happened in twenty years to make me believe that it is impossible, although the enormous increase in commercialized entertainment has made the going more difficult.

People might think that a medium like television which counts its audiences nightly in terms of millions was creating this cultural unity. At the moment it is creating unity but not culture. Unfortunately you don't create culture by making ten million people watch the same programme in the evening and discuss it the next morning. It is at least a step forward that a stockbroker should be able to discuss the previous night's programmes with his gardener; but television has a long way to go before it recreates the conditions of the first Elizabethan age.

In 1957 television costs £2,000 an hour, and there are

two services in operation both hoping to be allowed to run a second programme. Already £4,000 an hour! For four quid a year the British public gets thousands of hours of highly expensive entertainment. The theatre is in competition with this—at fifteen shillings for a single decent seat, out of which for years it paid a third in tax. As a gesture towards what is usually admitted to be the 'cultural value' of the theatre, the Treasury grants the Arts Council of Great Britain about £100,000 a year to spend on helping the British theatre. £100,000 is the equivalent of what is spent in twenty-four hours, or about three days, on the combined television services.

In the light of such figures as this the so-called Industry of Entertainment seems to be pretty hopelessly out-manoeuvred.

What then is the answer? Surely to let the theatre speak with its own unmistakable voice. The theatre's voice is the drama; and what the best of the British drama consists of is something that I have tried to describe in this book.

Then let the drama speak. The point at issue is whether it has spoken, or is ever likely to speak, with sufficient urgency to ensure a flow of fifteen shillings in the face of competition from that flickery little screen in the corner of the room.

But we must let the drama speak, not suppress it when it speaks unpalatably. We must not cry out for the protection of the Lord Chamberlain when O'Casey lets off a broadside about Communism, or shout 'Catholic propaganda' at the author of *Everyman*, or 'He's no dramatist' when Shaw offends our academic prejudices. What I think has emerged from this book is that great drama is the

XXIV
Arms and the Man at the New Theatre

XXV Sean O'Casey

XXVI (Below) Sean O'Casey in 1953

eruption of a moment in the conscience of mankind. The voice of drama is a passion, a conviction, a fury, a joy, a vision.

Have we not seen some wonderful examples of the creative impulse at work—and of its variety?

It may be quite simply the Christian faith which gave the tremendous breadth and drive to the *Corpus Christi plays,* to *The Castle of Perseverance,* and *Everyman*; it may be the vision of human grandeur that excited Marlowe, or the wide range of human experience that gave Shakespeare his extraordinary breadth and stature; it may be an ideal of social behaviour such as interested Dryden (in his heroic plays at any rate) or the love of watching the endless subtle interplay between men and women that fascinated Congreve. It may be pleasure in nothing more profound than trumping up a story to make people laugh—for perhaps we can set the ideal of Sheridan no higher than that, or the intense delight in his own craftsmanship that clearly fascinated Pinero; it may spring from the deep moral convictions that make that exquisite humorist, Bernard Shaw, one of the most serious writers who has ever lived, or the passionate belief in the beauty and splendour of man which animates O'Casey's plays. The impulse to write a play may come from any or all of these emotions and as many more as there are men and women who have set pen to paper.

Surely we are betraying our intellectual freedom if we ban the theatre to anyone with such visions, passions and convictions because they outrage our sensibilities, challenge our prejudices, or shake our indifference?

Surely we resign it just as surely if we shut our ears to the authentic voice of the theatre and listen only to gentle

12

English comedies and noisy American musicals in which
nothing erupts but a varying amount of sensuality and
shindy?

Notes on the Illustrations

I   In recent years the City of York has revived its magnificent
cycle of plays and had them performed, in a shortened version, against the ruins of St Mary's Abbey. The setting is
particularly appropriate since modern scholars think that most
of the plays may have been written by a monk of this abbey.
The authorities of York have reminded us of the processional
manner in which the plays were originally performed with a
single play given from a 'reconstructed pageant'. Here you see
the boys of the Archbishop Holgate's Grammar School performing the *Play of the Exodus* in the summer of 1957. In
medieval times there would doubtless have been a far greater
press of citizens surrounding the pageant and listening to the
actors. In certain countries predominantly Catholic, such as
Spain, the Festival of Easter is still celebrated with processions. Tableaux of Biblical scenes, mounted on waggons, with
figures often much larger than life made by people of surrounding villages are still hauled through the streets by teams
of men. I have searched in vain for a picture of the kind of
royal 'Entry' that Lydgate describes so vividly in his poem
about the entry of Henry VI into London, or the characters in
a Corpus Christi procession which he describes in another
poem. The annual Lord Mayor's procession through the City
of London is the nearest thing to be seen in England.

II   During the fifteenth century, the great period of the
medieval drama, people were especially haunted by the fear

of death, and the manner in which nobleman and peasant, rich and poor, were all struck down, often when least expecting it. Death was to them the great leveller. Sermons were given on the subject, some people think with mimed scenes going on at the same time. Poems were written on what was called the Dance of Death and illustrated. This is one of a series of forty-one woodcuts which Hans Holbein made in the fifteen-twenties. If you read W. H. Auden's satirical play *The Dance of Death* you will see how a modern poet has treated the same subject with Death depicted as a dancer.

III *Everyman* was rediscovered for the general public by William Poel who produced it in 1901. William Poel, one of the great producers of modern times, made it his life's work to produce the plays of Shakespeare and of the Elizabethan dramatists on stages, and in a manner, approximating as nearly as possible to their first productions. *Everyman,* though not an Elizabethan play, was his greatest success. Here you see the figure of Death. Why do you think it has become customary since Holbein to depict Death with a drum?

IV In 1949 I produced *Everyman* for the Children's Theatre. This is a photograph of the first entry of Death who, beneath his cloak, which he threw off on accosting Everyman, was dressed to suggest a skeleton. We were permitted to give performances of the play in the cathedrals of Norwich and Peterborough. In this we were luckier than William Poel who was refused permission to produce it in Lincoln Cathedral where an original manuscript of the play was treasured.

V The Moralities of the 15th and 16th centuries were given on open-air stages at fairs, markets, and wherever crowds of people were to be found. This portion of a large picture by the Dutch painter Pieter Balten gives a vivid impression of the conditions under which the early professional companies had to perform on their little improvised stages. It is not very difficult to see why they were sometimes driven to introduce dirty jokes and fireworks to hold the attention of their audiences.

VI   The early professional companies were sometimes invited to give performances of Moralities and Interludes in the house of some nobleman who loved the drama. Although this beautiful print shows a group of ladies and gentlemen dancing, and not actors, it gives an idea of the scene when one of these companies gave a performance in front of members of the household, many of whom must have watched from the galleries that are often to be found in Tudor houses. It also shows the kind of costumes that might well have been worn at the first performances of *Everyman*.

VII   Although there still exist many of the beautiful designs which Inigo Jones made for Jacobean Masques I have searched in vain for a picture of a Masque actually being performed in the improvised theatre of some great mansion. This engraving shows a kind of processional 'triumph' such as was very popular in Italy at the time of the Renaissance. It is taking place in the courtyard of a great palace with the audience packed on a temporary scaffolding. This might well be a celebration of a naval victory. The techniques used in such sumptuous spectacles were often copied by English designers and architects such as Inigo Jones.

VIII   This panoramic view of Elizabethan London from a contemporary print shows the Globe Theatre near the bank of the river about a quarter of the way across the picture from the left. It can be recognized by the flag. The Theatre and the Curtain were roughly due north of London Bridge.

IX   It is interesting to compare Plate VIII with this reconstruction of Elizabethan London that was made by Roger Furse for the film of *Henry V*. The Bear Garden and the Globe can be seen in the foreground. You will realize how close these two places of entertainment were to each other. In this picture the Theatre and the Curtain would be directly above and perhaps a little to the left of the Globe.

X   Here is an Elizabethan engraving of the Globe Theatre itself. I think we can assume that when a performance was taking place there was a good deal more activity around the theatre than the artist has shown here. But he was probably more interested in the theatre building than in people. It is computed that the Globe held something in the region of two thousand spectators. Since it was an open-air theatre and performances were given regularly throughout the winter from at least September until June—and in Elizabethan times the Thames was frozen over more than once—one wonders how the actors held the attention of their audiences at all.

XI   Here is a reconstruction of the interior of the Globe from the film of *Henry V*. It shows very clearly the proximity of the actors to the 'groundlings' standing round the stage in the pit. This picture does suggest the vigour of those early performances but it is a little difficult to reconcile the general roughness with the reports of visitors to London who all testified to the magnificence of the city's theatres.

XII—XV   Four great men of the theatre: Inigo Jones, Ben Jonson, John Dryden and William Congreve. It is extremely difficult to know how far an historical portrait can be taken as a likeness and how much the artist has intruded his own view of his subject's character; but I think the anonymous painter of Jonson, and Sir Anthony van Dyck (who painted Jones), have not disguised the fact that their subjects were a couple of irascible and headstrong fellows for all their genius. The portraits of Dryden and Congreve were done by Sir Godfrey Kneller. In this period a certain conventional flattery was usual. Dryden is given the Olympian splendour befitting a poet laureate. But even if the portraits don't tell us much about the two men we get a feeling of the style and dignity of the period, the proud set of the men's heads with their splendid wigs and elegant clothes, all of which is a part of the 'manners' depicted in the plays.

XVI   This famous print of the screen scene from *The School for Scandal* gives a vivid idea of the stage of Drury Lane in the early years of Sheridan's management. Some critics point out that the stage-boxes enabled the actors to keep in contact with their audience, but Colley Cibber, writing earlier in the century, complains that they pushed the actors farther and farther 'up-stage' and so away from the main body of the audience, with a marked loss of clarity. As a matter of fact until 1763 members of the public had been allowed actually to sit and stand on the stage during performances; but Garrick had put a stop to this abuse. For an enthralling book on the behaviour of audiences in the Georgian theatre see V. C. Clinton-Baddeley's *All Right on the Night*.

XVII   This charming contemporary print shows the outside of Sheridan's Drury Lane, together with the elegant dress of the gentry, their beautifully proportioned carriages, and a 'chair' in which they were conveyed over the rough dirty roads.

XVIII   A contemporary print of the disastrous destruction

of Drury Lane by fire in 1809 which ended Sheridan's extraordinarily long career as a theatre manager.

XIX   Compare this picture of a production of *As You Like It* by Charles Kean at the Princess's Theatre (near Oxford Circus) in the eighteen-fifties with the interior of Drury Lane shown in Plate XVI (and Drury Lane of the same period was not so different). The whole thing has been blown up. The audience is far bigger. The stage-boxes have gone. There is an enormous orchestra pit full of musicians, separating the actors from their audience. Behind the actors the castle of Duke Frederick, painted in the fashionable neo-Gothic style, is equally portentous. It is small wonder that in order to make their presence felt above acres of scenery and a hefty orchestra, and in an enormous auditorium, the actors had to develop a strong expressive style of playing that often became grotesque and bombastic. How must a delicate pastoral like *As You Like It* have suffered under these conditions! (The two women to the front of the stage are certainly Rosalind and Celia who have to comment on the fight of the two men. Music was used as commonly in the theatre then as it is in films today.)

XX   The central figure in this photograph is Sir George Alexander who presented at the St James's Theatre many of Pinero's greatest successes. This is a scene from a play by Pinero's contemporary, Alfred Sutro. The other actor is Matheson Lang. By this time (1907) great progress had been made in naturalistic acting, but the intense theatricalism of the actors' poses is still apparent.

XXI   Here is Sir Arthur Pinero in middle-age, photographed in his flat among the typical bric-a-brac of the period.

XXII   This amusing sequence of photographs shows Harley Granville Barker and Lillah McCarthy, whom he afterwards married, in scenes from the first production of Bernard Shaw's *Man and Superman*. The sixth picture shows that excellent actor Edmund Gwenn who together with Lewis Casson made his reputation in the play. It also made Shaw's reputation as the most daring, witty, and original, dramatist of the day. In Granville Barker Shaw had an interpreter, both as actor and producer, of unusual sensibility. Although the two men had wholly different attitudes to the drama, Barker erring on the side of subtlety while Shaw admired a more ferocious style, they seem to have complemented each other ideally. If you compare this photograph with Plate **XXIII** you will see that Barker made himself up to look like Shaw thereby identifying the revolutionary views of John Tanner in the play with those of the author.

XXIII   Here is a photograph of Bernard Shaw attending a meeting in 1896 to protest against a visit of the Czar of Russia to this country. Though still to make his reputation the picture shows that his striking appearance together no doubt with his original ideas and his trenchant way of delivering them drew the delighted attention of all who were standing near him. The picture emphasizes that Shaw was not an armchair socialist but a tireless and active supporter of social reform.

XXIV   In 1947 *Arms and the Man* was produced by the company of the Old Vic at the New Theatre. Laurence Olivier and Ralph Richardson, both of whom are to be seen in this photograph, were two of the directors of the company during one of its most brilliant periods. Raina, played by Margaret Leighton, can be seen with the two men. *Arms and the Man* was the second of Shaw's plays to be staged (1894). It shared the bill with an early play by another great Irish writer, *Land of Heart's Desire* by W. B. Yeats. Compare this picture with Plate XX. In the character of Sergius Shaw satirizes the theatrical romanticism which had been the stock-in-trade of English drama for over a century. The actor-managers were never very happy with Shaw and it was many years before his plays were commercially successful.

XXV Sean O'Casey photographed at the time of the first production of *Juno and the Paycock.*

XXVI Here he is nearly thirty years later when his play *Purple Dust* was being rehearsed by Sam Wanamaker. This was in 1953. This photograph does justice to the unique combination of strength and gentility that compose O'Casey's character. For I do not think one can love humanity as deeply as O'Casey does without hating the enemies of happiness. I have never spent three more happy days than in the company of him and his family.

INDEX

A

Abbey Theatre, Dublin, 157-60

Actors, first professional, 53

Adam le Bossu (early French dramatist), 40

Allegory, medieval, 42

Alleyn, Edward (Elizabethan actor), 56

Anonymous medieval dramatists, possible identity of, 36-7

Apron-stage, Elizabethan, 80-1

Archer, William (dramatic critic), 21, 136

Audiences, changing nature of, 11-12, 174-6

—in the Elizabethan theatre, 93, 174

—in the Restoration theatre, 104, 113-115, 174

—in the 19th century, 133-4, 175

—in the 20th century, 175

Authorship of Elizabethan plays, 63-4

B

Baker, George Pierce (American critic), 20, 136

Bale, John (author of *King John*), 52

Ballad operas in the 18th century, 122, 125

Bancroft, Sir Squire (19th century actor-manager), 132

Bath in the 18th century, 122

Betterton, Thomas (17th century actor-manager), 115, 120-1

Bible, stories from dramatized, 26, 28, 31, 37, 41

British Broadcasting Corporation, 19, 176

Browning, Robert (author of *Dramatist Personae*), 131

Boys' Companies, Elizabethan, 93

Burbage, Cuthbert, 56, 69

—James (Elizabethan actor), 54, 56

—Richard (Elizabethan actor), 56, 57, 69, 85

Byron, Lord (author of *Cain*), 131

C

Cambridge University, interest in drama at, 55-6

Cathedrals, building of and drama in, 23-5, 41

Castle of Perseverance, The (anonymous morality play), 177

—described and quoted, 44-6

—original staging of, 44

Chapman, George (Elizabethan dramatist), 13; collaboration on *Eastward Ho*, 93

Chartres Cathedral, 24

Chekhov, Anton (Russian dramatist), 10

Chester cycle of plays, 29, 30

—Chester play of *The Deluge*, 32

Civil War, England at the time of, 104

Classical authors, study of, 54, 58, 110

Collier, Jeremy (Restoration divine and pamphleteer), author of *A Short View of the Profaneness and Immorality of the English Stage*, 117-8

Condell, Henry (British actor and editor), 69-70

Congreve, William (dramatist), 13, 123, 125, 128, 143, 177, 183

—arrives in London and meets Dryden, 115

—*The Double Dealer*, 115

—*Love for Love*, 14, 116, 117

—*The Mourning Bride*, 115

—*The Old Bachelor*, 115

—*The Way of the World*, 115-7-8

—as a satirist, 116

—his natural gaiety, 116

—his ambitions and failure, 116-7

—texts of his plays, 118

Cornwall, medieval drama from, 29

Corpus Christi, Festival of, 26, 35, 38, 41, 44, 52, 177

—celebration of in England and France, 29